An Illustrated Guide to

Loving a
Soccer Fan

An Illustrated Guide to

Loving a Soccer Fan

*A Lighthearted Playbook to Connect with
the World's Most Serious Obsession*

Emberlite & Co.

LUZ AURORA ARAMBURO

Published by Emberlite & Co.

San Diego, California

ISBN (Paperback): 978-1-971133-00-3

ISBN (eBook): 978-1-971133-01-0

First edition

Printed in the United States of America

Ross and Alberto, thank you for helping me pretend I understood the Super Bowl. You gave me an idea.

To my customers — soccer fans and anti-fans alike — for being generous with feedback and ideas.

A thousand heads are better than one.

Author's Note

The Pelé-Maradona debate will outlive all of us. Pelé scored over 1,200 career goals and won three World Cups with Brazil, while Maradona only lifted one; he scored 259 club goals and became immortal for his "Hand of God" and 1986 solo run against England — two legends, one endless debate.

Oh no, did we lose you already? None of that really matters. What you care about is your partner, and we do too. Who says sports have to be about stats and fun facts? Not us. This book isn't here to turn you into "one of the guys." He has plenty of those. The goal is to connect with your partner on a deeper, more meaningful level. This guidebook provides insight into what makes soccer such a vital part of his world and how to stay connected without losing yourself in the process. Welcome to the world of soccer obsession. If you're dating a die-hard fan, this guide is your secret weapon. You'll learn just enough to hold your own — how the game works, what to say during a match, how to survive a World Cup, and how to turn small talk into connection. This book isn't trying to make you love soccer. It's here to help you decode it — emotionally, practically, and relationally. Just become someone who gets it — or at least knows how to pretend with charm.

Again, this is about navigating connections in modern relationships. Many of us didn't have the privilege to see emotional health modeled in our homes. Others grew up in homes with great relationships and now feel pressure to copy them exactly. Either

way, your relationship doesn't need to replicate your parents' version. Relationships today look different from 10, 20, or 30 years ago. What was once "normal" might now feel like a red flag — and what feels healthy now might evolve again in a decade. That's okay, we are growing and changing as a species. The point is, you get to build something that reflects your needs, values, and growth.

Psychologist Dr. John Gottman found that the most significant predictors of a relationship's success aren't grand gestures or flawless communication — it's the small, everyday moments of turning toward each other instead of away. Those tiny "bids for connection" — a comment, a glance, a joke — are what keep love alive. Miss enough of them, and distance creeps in. Add criticism, contempt, defensiveness, or stonewalling (what Gottman calls the "Four Horsemen"), and even the strongest couples begin to crumble.

And that's why I chose soccer as the lens for this book. Not because you need to become a fan, but because sports are a common point of contention in relationships. It's something couples argue about every season — time, attention, priorities, emotions, mood swings, screen time, fantasy leagues, and fan culture. So instead of giving you more theories about what you should do, this book provides you with real-life phrases, tools, and tiny conversational shifts that turn something couples usually fight about into something that brings you closer.

This book is here to help you spot those little bids for connection — during game season or beyond — and to turn toward each other instead of away. Because love, like the game, is won in small plays, not just big moments.

This is not a rulebook. It's a resource. Take what fits. Leave what doesn't. Trust your gut. Speak up when something doesn't feel right. And if nothing else, know this: you are not the only one trying to make sense of why a grown man is screaming at a TV.

Table of Contents

I.
the passion
& your
playbook

The Passion

"In his life, a man can change wives, political parties, or religions, but he cannot change his favorite soccer team."
~ Eduardo Hughes Galeano.

Most passionate soccer fans have been loyal to their team since they can remember. These teams are a part of their upbringing and identity. It's an ancient tradition, merely a modern take on knights jousting or gladiators fighting. This is their ritual. And, like all rituals, it anchors them.

Women will vent to friends, family, or even strangers. Men? They gather and scream at a referee who can't hear them.

For better or worse, this is one of the few socially acceptable ways men are allowed to feel their full range of emotions. Some jump for joy; others cry (yes, happy and sad tears). Somehow, society decided that yelling at a TV screen is a valid emotional outlet — men took it and ran.

Why does HE love soccer?
What does HE get out of it?

Proceed with caution, trust your judgement, and see if you can poke it out of him. Your guy might be the kind of person who lights up when someone asks the origin of his passion. He could reminisce about kicking the ball around with his father or the kid next door. This could be the perfect opportunity to learn a bit about his upbringing.

He might also be the type who does not want to discuss his feelings about soccer. Many men simply love being able to escape from reality for two hours at a time. There is something psychologically necessary about being able to disconnect from your life troubles and give your mind (and emotions) a break. Following his soccer team might be it for him. For you, it might be reality TV, shop therapy, working out, or reading.

Checking out from time to time prevents stress, which could lead to:

- **Decision fatigue** — making simple choices becomes overwhelming.

- **Impaired focus and memory** — your brain struggles to retain or process new information.

- **Mental exhaustion** — constant input with no rest leads to brain fog or shutdown.

- **Emotional reactivity** — snapping over small things, mood swings, or outbursts.

- **Withdrawal** — pulling away from loved ones to avoid more stimulation.

- **Decreased empathy** — too maxed out to care deeply or respond with patience.

- **Increased reliance on coping mechanisms** — like alcohol, screen time, or emotional eating.

- **Resentment buildup** — no space to decompress and no bandwidth for connection.

- **Escalating conflict** — partners misinterpret or absorb each other's stress.

- **Insomnia or restless sleep** — your nervous system stays "on," even at night.

- **Tension headaches, jaw clenching, digestive issues** — chronic stress shows up physically.

- **Compromised immune function** — stress hormones suppress your body's defenses.

- **Lower self-confidence** — feeling like you're constantly behind or not handling life well.

- **Disconnection from joy** — things that used to excite you now feel like chores.

Still, soccer is not the ONLY way to check out. And if he wants to check out for most of his time, then there may be an underlying need. Explore this topic further in the 'Identity' section (page 43).

How to Lose a Guy in 10 Plays

1. **Call his passion a "Waste of Time."**

By that logic, so is every silly conversation you've ever had with friends, every fictional show you've binge-watched, and every hour lost to TikTok. But these things all serve the same purpose: a brief escape from the heavy realities of life.

2. **Become the soccer guru.**

He doesn't need you to be a know-it-all about soccer. You cannot out-love or out-know his hobby — it messes with the ecosystem. Let him be the expert in this arena. Aim to know a maximum of 75% of what he knows. You're learning for connection, not competition. You wouldn't want him mansplaining the Kardashians to you, so don't try to out-coach him on soccer.

3. **Pretend you like the game when you actually don't.**

This is not the time to fake it. It's as annoying as him tagging along on a shopping spree, whining about when you'll be done, and saying, "Yeah, it looks great" to every single outfit you try on. Give it an honest try, but if you'd rather poke out your eyes, refer to page 36 for ideas on how to disengage during his games. Remember that you're allowed to dislike things he loves.

4.

Tell his friends to use coasters for their beers.

If you know that he's hosting and your furniture is delicate, then have him prep by getting a soccer-themed plastic tablecloth or beer holders: cold drinks, dry tables, zero drama.

5.

Schedule date night during game night so he has to prove you're his priority.

Forcing him to "prove you're the priority" is a lose-lose situation. If you know he's passionate about something, create a schedule together that honors both of your needs rather than pressuring him to make a choice. You deserve to be prioritized — but the healthiest proof comes from consistency, not tests. If you continue to feel he needs to prove you're a priority, that feeling usually points to something deeper. It might be on his end or yours; talk it through with a therapist or even a trusted friend to see what is really lying underneath. For a deeper dive, see the section "Priorities & Schedule" (page 66) to navigate these conversations.

6.

Ask questions throughout the whole game.

You'll have to read the room on this one. Some men love explaining their obsession if their partner has genuine curiosity. Others want to zero in on the game and forget they are sitting next to someone on a couch. Learn which type you've got. If you can't tell, just... ask him...

7.

Give him something to do during an important game so he won't be able to watch.

You wouldn't want him asking you to wash dishes while you're in the middle of a manicure. Game time is his "me time." It may look different than yours, but it's just as necessary for his sanity. If you need him to pick up his slack, check page 197 for tasks he can do during a non-essential game (and when he doesn't have friends over).

8.

Make him "earn" his game time.

There's a big difference between agreeing together on when he'll watch and giving him a chore checklist he has to finish before kick-off — one is partnership, the other is parenting. You might be a sexy mama, but being his mama is not attractive. *Freud rolls in his grave.

9.

Remind him that it is "Just a game" when his team loses.

Yes, they're strangers in uniforms — but he feels part of the team. Losses can hit hard. On the bright side, it means he's in touch with his emotions. On the downside, he may need to work on regulating them. Ask how much time he needs to decompress — just agree on a cutoff point (30 minutes? 1 hour?) so his mood doesn't hijack your whole day. Check out the Emotional Regulation section (page 54) for more tips on navigating this conversation.

10.

Mock his game-day rituals.

Maybe he wears a "lucky" jersey, or sits in the same spot on the couch every single game. It may look ridiculous, but to him it's a "serious strategy." Teasing can quickly turn into disrespect if you're not careful. Think of it like him poking fun at your 20-step skincare routine — it looks weird to him, but it matters to you.

Finding Your Playbook

Roles, Support, and Love Languages

Loving a soccer fan is not a one-size-fits-all experience. You don't have to become a die-hard, memorize stats, or pretend to care about corner kicks to stay connected. But it is worth noticing how you naturally show up versus what kind of support the relationship actually needs.

Think of this as your relationship playbook: the roles you might step into, the ways you can offer support, and the "love languages" that help keep things balanced. A strong connection fulfills both of you; it doesn't cater to one person.

Important note: These ideas aren't official therapy models — they're practical, real-life patterns inspired by psychological principles. Translation: they're tools, not diagnoses; frameworks, not fixed rules. If something helps, keep it. If it doesn't, toss it. **You decide the strategy.** That's how a playbook works.

The Partner Roles

You'll probably find yourself in one (or more) of these throughout the soccer season. None is "better" than the others — just different strategies for staying sane while he's glued to the screen. Switch between them depending on your energy level and what both of you need at that moment.

The Effective Disengager: You choose how you want to spend that window — not out of avoidance, but out of intention. Schedule your mani/pedi, a girls' night out, errands, or a spa session. If you have kids, this is the perfect window for mom-and-kid adventures.

You thrive in providing Space — respecting independence without guilt trips.

Resources to play smarter: Disengaging Activities - page 36.

The Supportive Fan: You can sit next to him, scroll occasionally, and cheer at random intervals. Do it because you want to share the moment, not because you feel obligated to perform interest. Tag along to games, join him at the sports bar, or follow the drama at home. Even if you're uninvested in the score, the chaos, the food, or the people-watching is fascinating.

You thrive in providing Emotional Support — being present without performing.

Resources to play smarter: Going to the Game - page 27; The Basics - page 99; The Players - page 106 ; The World Cup - page 114.

The Hostess: Turning your home into the go-to match spot creates connection without forcing conversation — everyone's focused on the game, but you're building community. Hosting is powerful when you choose it, not when you feel drafted into it. Master the essentials (nachos, wings, or a signature cocktail) and make it your own. Hosting can be less about impressing guests and more about creating an atmosphere where both of you can enjoy yourselves. You can also use these games as a built-in reason to test new recipes.

You thrive in providing Social and Practical Support.

Resources to play smarter: the World Cup - page 114; Hosting - page 189.

The Shopaholic: Turns fandom into fashion. Think of it as accessorizing affection: matching jerseys, scarves, and lucky socks. Deck yourself, your partner, and the living room in team swag.

You thrive in providing Encouragement — celebrating passion with flair.

Resources to play smarter: Gift Guide - page 195.

The Enabler: Plans viewing parties, buys the face paint, surprises him with season tickets, and invents drinking games every time someone dives dramatically. You're here for the chaos — and the fun.

> You thrive in providing Social support and Acts of Service. Just keep it light — not co-dependent.
>
> *Resources to play smarter*: Yelling at the TV - page 25; Gift Guide - page 195.

The Memory Maker: Turns soccer into adventure: road trips to stadiums, themed date nights, lucky snacks, travel goals, or silly rituals. For you, it's not about the game — it's about creating stories together.

> You thrive in providing Growth and Quality Time — shared experiences that make love feel like a team sport.
>
> *Resources to play smarter*: Going to the Game - page 27; Tailgating; - page 28; The World Cup - page 114.

Support Styles

Now that you've identified which role you fall into during games, let's zoom out. Roles are situational, but support styles dig deeper—they're the ways you naturally show up in the relationship, soccer or not.

Support is one of those words everyone uses but rarely defines — and that's where relationships start to unravel. We assume our version is universal: "I'd want him to listen, so I'll listen." Or, "I'd want space, so I'll give him space." However, people give and receive support in different ways. What feels loving to one person can feel dismissive to another. Real connection comes from knowing the difference, not assuming yours and his look the same.

Here are seven kinds of support — and how to tell which ones actually work for both of you.

Emotional: Listening, validating, or holding space — not fixing.

Sit next to him after a tough loss, no words required. He may want to process in silence.

Say, "That looked rough — I get why you're upset," instead of, "It's just a game."

Remember: Sometimes we jump to problem-solving because silence is awkward. Validation doesn't mean agreement — it means understanding.

Practical: Tag-teaming life so both of you can breathe.

You grab dinner during his big match, and he does when you're on deadline.

Splitting chores so no one's keeping score.

Remember: Practical support works best when it's mutual — think partnership, not project management.

Social: Showing interest in each other's worlds (without pretending to love them).

You join him for one game; he joins you for brunch with your friends.

He cheers for your promotion party; you learn who his favorite players are.

Remember: Curiosity counts as connection. Pretending is performative; curiosity is a sign of respect.

Growth: Reinforce personal growth, even when it's uncomfortable.

Say, "I'm proud of you for trying therapy," not "Wow, finally."

Name patterns gently, "You get quiet after losses — want to talk about that?" Celebrate

progress, not perfection. "I want both of us to keep growing — not just getting by."

Remember: Supporting growth is long-term love. It's not fixing each other or freezing each other in time; it's walking beside one another while you both evolve.

Space: Respecting each other's alone time without guilt trips. He watches soccer; you dive into your book, bath, or binge-watch your favorite show.

Neither of you gets defensive about needing time to recharge.

"You do your thing, I'll do mine — we'll regroup later."

Remember: Space isn't rejection — it's oxygen.

Encouragement: Words and gestures that make someone feel seen, safe, and appreciated.

Say, " I love that you're so passionate about this " instead of "You're obsessed."

Send a halftime text: 'Hope your team pulls through. Have fun with the guys.'

Or say "I appreciate how much this matters to you."

Remember: For some people, words are fuel. If that's him, use them generously.

Boundary: Loving someone while keeping yourself intact.

Say, "I know this game matters, but I also want us to have dinner before 9 PM."

Set time limits after losses so moods don't dominate the night.

"I want us both to enjoy this without burning out."

Remember: Boundaries aren't punishment. They are structures that keep your connections safe.

Support goes both ways. You're not auditioning for the role of 'perfect partner.' You're setting the tone for a relationship where your needs carry equal weight.

Soccer Love Languages

Every couple has a rhythm — the small ways love shows up between goals, arguments, and everyday chaos. Roles are moment-by-moment choices. Support styles are long-term patterns. Love languages are the emotional glue that makes those choices feel meaningful. Knowing each other's love language is like learning your team's favorite formation. The Five Love Languages can be a helpful starting point because they prompt people to think about what makes them feel cared for. But they're not the whole story. Real relationships are more complex than five categories, and most of us express love in more than one way, depending on the moment, stress level, or dynamic.

So treat love languages like a tool, not a diagnosis: useful, but not an all-encompassing fix. They're a doorway into connection, not the entire house.

Physical Touch: You don't have to be fully engaged in the game — even just putting your feet on his lap while you scroll your phone can fill his cup. Hug it out when his team loses, or maybe comfort him with more than a hug...

Words of Affirmation: Compliment him, not just his team. "You know more about this lineup than half the commentators." Or, "I love how passionate you get about this."

Acts of Service: Prepping snacks or clearing the table before kickoff isn't servitude — it's thoughtfulness. Get something off his to-do list so he can enjoy the game more thoroughly. But put your oxygen mask on first, don't get into his to-do list if you're overwhelmed with yours.

Quality Time: This guy will definitely want you to spend some time on the couch watching the game with him. But even better, upgrade the sofa for some stadium seats. Building memories together will mean the most to him.

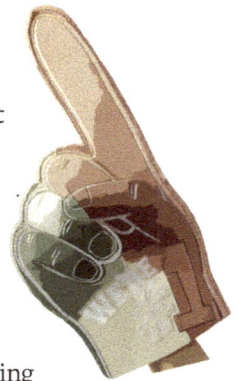

Gifts: From jerseys to face paint to tickets, gifts keep the spirit alive. Go all out with themed surprises or create funny traditions, like a "lucky snack" you only eat on game days.

Your Connection Game Plan

Develop a game plan: Combine your Love Language with his Support Style. If you combine Space Support and Acts of Service, prepare snacks, and then disappear. If you combine Emotional Support and Words of Affirmation, stay close and offer encouragement. You're not managing his emotions — but *you* get to decide how you want to give and receive love.

Your needs matter just as much as his — don't shrink them.

None of these roles, styles, or languages makes you a better or worse partner. They're just tools — ways to build awareness and meet each other where you're at. Remember, this is a team sport: you don't have to play the same position, but you do have to play on the same side.

If you want to translate these ideas beyond soccer and into the rest of your relationship, start with *The 5 Love Languages* by Gary Chapman — it's an easy read that explains why even the best intentions sometimes miss the mark.

If you want to explore the deeper forces behind love — attachment, communication patterns, emotional regulation, the stuff that actually predicts long-term relationship health — try:

Attached by Amir Levine & Rachel Heller

The Seven Principles for Making Marriage Work by Dr. John Gottman

II.
surviving
soccer season

Yelling at the TV

I f this loud, chaotic tradition gets under your skin, don't try to quiet it. Instead, **join it**. Channel your irritation toward the other team. Yell right along with him. It might surprise you how therapeutic yelling at a TV can be. You'll feel your own stress melt into the roar of the crowd. The following phrases function best when you have a partner who also yells at the TV. Here are a few catch-all phrases you can use and when to use them.

YOUR CUE	WHAT TO YELL!
After a tense moment, if your partner is pissed off. Don't calm him down, be OUTRAGED together!	Come on! What was that?
A player misses an easy shot.	That was wide open! I can't believe he missed that!
Your team scores.	GOOOOOAAAAAALLLLL!!!! WHAT A GOAL! Did you see that?
The ref makes a call against his team.	What game is he even watching? Did they buy him out?
The other team is stalling or faking an injury (remember to support your team's drama, we call that strategy).	Get up, drama queen! This isn't Broadway!
It is halftime, and your team is losing.	It's okay, there's still time on the clock. They just need to pick it up.
The other team scores for the first time.	Okay. Lucky shot. That's the only one they're getting.
The referee is reviewing the video, and it is taking forever (this only happens in crucial games / close calls).	It's not brain surgery! Just make the call already!
A player on the opposing team gets a yellow card.	That's right, walk away! You're lucky it wasn't red.
A substitute comes on for your team, and the fans don't like him.	Him? Really? Why not just play with 10 men?
Your team is about to score a goal that would tie the game.	COME ON! COME ON! We need that equalizer!!
The referee is deliberating on whether the opposing team committed an infraction.	Where is the yellow? That was definitely a yellow!

Going to the Game

Game Day Fit

You NEED to be comfy! Crop tops are fair game as long as you can move without a wardrobe malfunction. There will be steep stairs and lots of sideways shimmying past strangers to reach your seat, so it's not the most mini-skirt- or dress-friendly environment.

Color coding: Sometimes opposing teams share the same colors. Which is why each team has two different jerseys. Look up the color your team will be representing that day and ensure you match it. Don't accidentally blend in with the enemy.

*** *Whatever you do, don't wear the other team's colors!*

Check the weather! These are long events, and it can get chilly at night. This is a good time to borrow his oversized team jacket or cap. He'll love seeing you in it and supporting both him and the team. But plan this ahead of time! Hopefully, you're with the kind of guy who will offer his jacket when you're shivering, but don't make him freeze due to your poor planning.

PURSE CHECK!

Each stadium has its own policy for purses. Many require clear bags or handbags of a specific size. Check your particular stadium's policy.

☐ IDs (for drinking)

☐ Cards (many stadiums have a no cash policy)

☐ Your phone (for pics)

☐ Sunglasses (daytime)

☐ Chapstick (for kissing)

Getting There

Parking is a nightmare — getting in, getting out, and paying for it. If public transit takes you straight to the stadium, take the win (and save the planet while you're at it). If crowds stress you out, consider arriving early and slipping out before the stampede. Bonus: public transportation means you both get to drink. However you end up getting there, a match is always worth the mission.

Tailgating

Tailgating is an American sports tradition that predates soccer's serious adoption in the U.S. It's essentially the country's way of saying, "Can we start our play date in the parking lot? All of my other fan friends are already here." As soccer grew in popularity in the United States, fans borrowed the ritual — grills, coolers, lawn chairs, and portable speakers — and adapted it for match day.

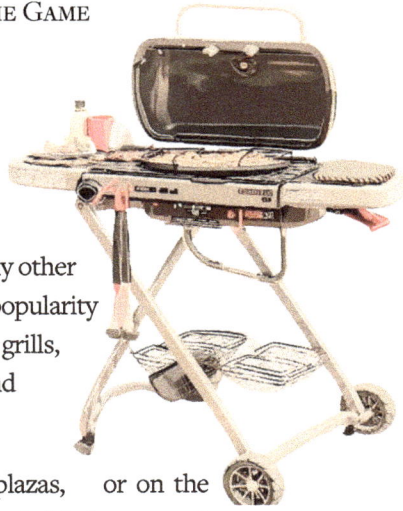

In most parts of the world, fans gather in pubs, plazas, or on the streets. In America? They set up a mini block party behind someone's SUV and call it culture. Both are fun. Just don't show up with a grill at a stadium in Spain and wonder why security is staring at you. For some people, tailgating is the main event. It can stretch your outing by 2–3 hours, turning it into an outdoor picnic with friends, music, food, and whatever level of chaos your group brings.

Bonus: Stadium food and drinks are expensive, and tailgating saves you from paying for the costly beer that tastes like regret. If this sounds like your scene, jump in. If not, no pressure — you can pregame elsewhere and meet the chaos inside. Tailgating, like everything else, is optional.

Tips for Introverts:
Bring one anchor friend and join the edge of the chaos
- Wear team colors — participation without conversation
- Offer to keep the snack table stocked
-

TAILGATE CHECKLIST	
☐ Finger-friendly food	☐ Trash bags (have some class)
☐ Grill - gas-powered. Check your stadium policy. Can't discard coals in parking lots.	☐ Chairs
	☐ Canopy
☐ Drinks	☐ Sunscreen
☐ Chest Cooler + Ice	☐ Hat or caps
☐ Bluetooth speaker for music	☐ Bug spray
	☐ Napkins/paper towels
	☐ Games (cornhole, cards)

When You Don't Want To Go

Not wanting to go doesn't make you unsupportive — it makes you human. You're allowed to love him and still not want to sit in a freezing stadium surrounded by grown men shouting at referees from 40 rows away. Here's an easy line to bow out: "I love how excited you are. I'm going to skip this one, but go have the best time." No over-explaining. No apology tour. Just clarity with kindness.

You can be emotionally present without freezing in a plastic seat. Try:

"Text me if something wild happens," or "Give me the recap after."

It says: I care about you. I just don't care for the seat I'd be sitting in. Explain where you're coming from: "In-person games are a lot for me. I'm happier cheering from home." This is emotional maturity, not avoidance. End on connection, not distance.

"When you're done, come over — I'll have snacks ready." Or, "I can join you in the after-party at the bar."

Things to avoid:

- Don't guilt-trip him for going.
- Don't get guilt-tripped for not going.
- Don't force yourself to go just to "be supportive" and then spend four hours annoyed.
- Don't pretend you're fine and then sulk later.

Your "no" should feel like a boundary, not a booby trap. Remember that skipping the game doesn't mean you're skipping him. It means you know your limits — that's part of adulting.

When You Weren't Invited

He tells you he's going "with the guys." It is not just about the game — it's about connecting with his friends. Men often tuck emotional bonding under something "culturally acceptable," such as sports. Women can call a friend and talk for three hours. Men need an external excuse: a team, a backyard project, a barbecue, a match, or a referee. This won't apply to every man, but it applies to a lot of them.

Before anything else, ask yourself: ***Why do I want to go?***

- Am I excited about the game itself?
- Am I feeling FOMO?
- Do I want time with him?
- Am I scared of being left out?
- Do I just not want to be alone while he's out having fun?

Honesty with yourself is essential. If the desire stems from a need for connection, then great! Consider scheduling something fun with him for that week (find date ideas on page 70). If it comes from anxiety, then pay attention to it and readjust accordingly: reach out to your friends, practice grounding techniques (page 200), or talk to someone who can help you sort through it (page 95).

Try to stay open: Support his excitement without attaching it to your worth. If this feeling is surprisingly intense, it might be tapping into something older than the relationship.

If it's a guys-only thing, let him have it. Men need male friendships just as much as you need your gals — it might just be harder for them to name it. Some people simply recharge best with their friends or on their own, and that preference deserves the same respect either way. The best relationships thrive on a blend of:

Together time

Separate time

Friendship time

Solo recharge time

If any of those become "off-limits," that's when it's time to look at the underlying emotional pattern — not the soccer match.

For the actual conversation: Lead with clarity, not wounded pride. You don't need to audition for a ticket. Try:

"I'd love to go, but if this is a guys-only night, just tell me so I'm not guessing. I want to be on the same page."

With this sentence, you say:

- ● I want to be there.

- ● I'm glad you have your people.

- ● I reinforce good communication and honesty.

- ● And yes — it also covers the "other women" question without you having to ask directly. There is nothing wrong with asking directly.

There is also a chance he simply didn't realize you wanted to go. Many men do not pick up on the subtleties of hints. Be clear, kind, and impossible to misinterpret.

If It's Not a Guys-Only Thing and Other Women Are Going

Request clarity, do not jump to conclusions. An emotionally mature man will explain. A good relationship can handle the conversation. And the best version of you will stay curious, not reactive. It's usually about communication, comfort, or boundaries he hasn't articulated yet. Gently but directly clarify what's really going on:

"I heard some of the other partners are going. Do you prefer I sit this one out? I want to understand the vibe and make sure it is not something else going on between us."

This tone does three things:

1. You are *not* accusing him.

2. You're giving him room to be honest.

3. You are calmly signaling that mixed messages don't work for you.

Now, what might actually be happening?

A. He genuinely didn't think about it.

Some people can be shockingly literal. If he didn't invite you, in his mind, it's "guys' night," even if other guys' partners got asked by their boyfriends. Not malicious — just not relationally attuned. He'll usually respond with: "Oh — I didn't know they were coming. Do you want to come too?"

B. He wants you there... but he's worried you won't enjoy it.

Some guys try to "protect" you from chaos, drunk energy, or a friend group that gets a little too rowdy and does not articulate it well. If that's the case, you can ease his worry:

"If you're worried I won't enjoy it, I promise I'll let you know. Just give me the option."

C. He's not sure how you fit into that friend dynamic yet.

It doesn't mean you're unwelcome. It could mean he is still learning how to blend his worlds. You can reassure him with:

"I don't have to be glued to your side. I'm happy to go, meet people, and let you socialize."

D. He actually didn't want you at this one — but didn't know how to say it.

If so, he needs to learn to express his needs honestly, not with excuses. You can model maturity without taking it personally. This shows emotional intelligence, not insecurity. This is about communication, not competition. Keep in mind that both parties need to nurture "together time." Not all day, every day. But if spending time together never happens, you're not growing as a couple. It is about patterns, not one-offs. Talk about it and do a pulse check on what you need from each other.

If exclusion becomes a pattern designed to keep you separate from his world, that *might* be a relationship issue.

Tools to cope with not being invited:

- **Anchor yourself:** "My value doesn't shrink because I wasn't invited."
- **Redirect energy:** Plan something for yourself — a girls night, a bath, a book, a hobby.
- **Stay open:** Support his excitement without attaching it to your worth.
- **Stay curious:** "Is this about connection for me, or about fear?"
- **Name your needs:** Calmly, without keeping score.

What doesn't work:

- Acting unbothered while internally stewing
- Saying "It's fine" when your energy says otherwise
- Showing up anyway just to prove a point
- Treating guy time like a threat or an insult

Skip the emotional acrobatics;
they drain both of you.

Disengaging Activities

Sometimes the best way to support him during a match is to help yourself. His "me time" doesn't require you to sit there bored out of your mind — you get to have your own playbook. Think of this as your freedom pass: choose what restores you, energizes you, or simply gets you out of his yelling radius.

Be Productive:

Start your 401 (k) or invest

Create a budget

Meal prep for the week

Take an online course

Write handwritten letters or cards

Work on a side hustle

Declutter and organize your space

Sell things on Poshmark / FB Marketplace

Return unwanted packages

Create a vision board

Learn a language, coding, or mixology

Plan upcoming trip

Schedule appointments (doctor, dentist)

Back up your phone photos

Update your resume / LinkedIn

Volunteer

Organize your closet

Be Creative:

Experiment with photography

Start a podcast or TikTok series

Start a journal or bullet journal

Knit or crochet

Make candles

Paint or watercolor

Learn a new recipe

Bake sourdough

Host a girls' night

Upcycle clothing

Practice a musical instrument

Write or journal

Try a DIY project

Rearrange a room

Try a new makeup look

Learn pottery

Make jewelry

Scrapbook

Garden

Me Time:

Go for a scenic drive, walk, or run

Take a fitness or yoga class

Go on a solo coffee date

Do a home workout challenge

Pamper your pet

Get a mani/pedi

Order your favorite takeout

Call loved ones

Use a face mask

Pair wine with a bubble bath

Buy yourself flowers

Do a hair treatment

Pluck your eyebrows

Get a wax

Go for a walk or run

Meditate

Join Your Couch Potato:

Do a digital declutter

Unsubscribe from junk emails

Listen to a podcast

Draw/paint

Read (with noise-cancelling headphones)

Shop online

Catch up on social media posts

Reply to ignored texts

Edit photos

Pinterest your next project

Play games or puzzles

Watch your show with headphones

III.
the emotional arena

Is Your Partner Out of Bounds?

Sustainable vs. Obsessive Fandom

A sustainable passion is linked with well-being, life satisfaction, and emotional resilience, while obsessive passion often aligns with anxiety, burnout, poor interpersonal functioning, and even depression. The problem is not soccer itself; it is simply an outlet for what is lying underneath. Obsessive behaviors typically indicate stress, unmet needs, or a lack of healthy coping skills — not a flaw in the partner.

A grounded fan can laugh at a loss, step away from a screen, and still prioritize you. Obsessive patterns often feel like you're in a relationship with the team, not the person. If your gut is telling you this feels more like an obsession than a hobby, you're probably picking up on obsessive patterns. Intensity alone isn't unhealthy — plenty of people are passionate, loud, or deeply invested without crossing a line. The difference isn't passion — it's rigidity. Sustainable and "harmonious" passion bends; obsessive passion breaks.

It's okay to set boundaries or even suggest a conversation with a therapist if it's affecting your well-being. Every single relationship will be different. These examples highlight common patterns found in relationships and help you identify what you both need to make *your* relationship work.

These are not clinical criteria — just unpolished wisdom to help you pay attention to the health of the dynamic, not the volume of the fandom.

Here's what a constructive partnership tends to look like — not perfectly, not all the time, but consistently enough that you both feel safe being vulnerable.

The best relationships aim to:

- **Work as a team** — same side, same goal.
- **Check in with each other's feelings**, even when you don't volunteer them.
- **Follow through** — if you say it, do it.
- **Protect and reinforce trust.**
- **Communicate honestly,** especially when it's uncomfortable.
- **Encourage happiness**, not jealousy or competition.
- **Support each other generously** — be cheerleaders, not critics.
- **View differences as complementary**, not annoying.
- **Prioritize quality time**, and respect independence.
- **Resolve conflict with the relationship in mind**, not the scoreboard.
- **Nurture intimacy**, emotionally and physically.
- **Show appreciation** in small ways, significant ways, and spontaneous ways.
- **Make space for growth**, and don't freeze each other in time.

Let's Talk About It

The best way to handle a confrontation is to *not* view it like a confrontation. You're not talking to your problem — you're talking with your partner. He's not the enemy. The issue is something you're facing together. The goal isn't to "win" the argument; it's to protect the connection. Here are some key rules of engagement to keep your conversations productive and helpful. This kind of conversation might not go perfectly the first time — and that's okay. If things get heated, suggest taking a break and revisiting the topic when you're both regulated again. That in itself is emotional progress.

1. Timing Is Everything

You are heard best when emotions are low, and everyone is calm, sober, and focused. Not mid-game, mid-fight, mid-drink, mid-dream, or mid-scroll.

2. Lead with Care, Not Criticism

Curiosity keeps the conversation open; criticism shuts it down. Swap "You always—" for "I've been feeling—." The second version invites him in; the first makes him defensive before you've finished your sentence.

> **GAME CHANGER**
>
> Sit next to him, not across from him. That slight shift can change the energy of the conversation. It creates emotional safety and reminds you both that you're on the same side— working to strengthen the relationship, not fighting each other.

3. Use Team Language

Collaborative language feels less threatening and invites a sense of partnership. It's not you versus him — it's *you two versus the issue.*

> "Can *we* figure this out together?"

> "I think *we* both want things to feel lighter and less tense."

4. Stick to Observations, Not Accusations

Focus on what you've seen or felt, not what you think he meant.

> "I've noticed we *argue more on game nights*."

> "I *feel shut out* when soccer becomes the only thing we talk about."

These statements create space for connection instead of conflict. Observations invite understanding; assumptions invite debate and argument.

5. Set Clear, Shared, and Reasonable Boundaries

Rather than vague requests, co-create clear expectations.

> "If things get tense, *can we call a time-out and regroup*?

> "If you need space, just *tell me* that — *don't disappear* mid-conversation."

Boundaries feel more supportive when they're co-created — not rules handed down. Boundaries aren't ultimatums — they're agreements you both refine over time.

6. Use Natural Consequences as Insight

Point to real-life examples between the two of you. Stay grounded in shared experience, not vague theory or lectures.

Example: "Last week, we had a rough night after the game, and the *tension stuck around all weekend*. That's *not how I want us to feel*."

Frame consequences as things you both experienced together, not something he 'caused'. Focusing the conversation on consequences keeps it focused on *what's actually happening*, rather than assumptions.

7. Keep the Focus on *Connection*

Remind him—and yourself—that this isn't about control. It's about protecting your connection and creating a better shared experience. Say this:

"This matters to me because *we matter* to me."

"I don't want this to *come between us*. I want to feel like *we're on the same team*."

Relationships aren't about perfect communication; they're about constant repair. You'll both fumble sometimes. The key is noticing when the tone shifts from connection to competition.

Remember: It takes two to tango, and two to create a healthy relationship.

As you read through the compilation of hallmark issues in relationships, **look out for issues that resonate with *your* behavior.** Check in with your partner and ask if it is affecting your dynamic.

Expanding Identity

Identities are not static — but it's not a free-for-all either. Identity evolves, shaped by life experiences, relationships, stress, culture, and self-reflection. The key here is whether it's balanced. A partner's love for soccer can be one piece of who they are — but if it becomes the only piece, then everything else gets squeezed out: your conversations, your plans, your sense of partnership.

Note: This is not about making him "less of a fan." It's about ensuring that his identity isn't overly dependent on a single source of meaning. Sometimes life gets chaotic, and people lean extra hard on one hobby for a season. That doesn't automatically mean there's a problem. You're looking for patterns, not one intense month.

How to Tell If It's a Problem

The Wheel of Life is a simple yet powerful visual tool used by coaches, mentors, and relationship experts to help individuals assess the balance of their life across different areas. Each "slice" of the wheel represents a part of life that contributes to overall life satisfaction and fulfillment.

You rate each area on a scale of 1 to 10, and see whether your life feels balanced — or if one area (say, soccer fandom) is taking up all the oxygen.

There are different versions of the wheel, but this one includes the following aspects of life:

Career / Business – Fulfillment, growth, and success in your work.

THE LIFE WHEEL

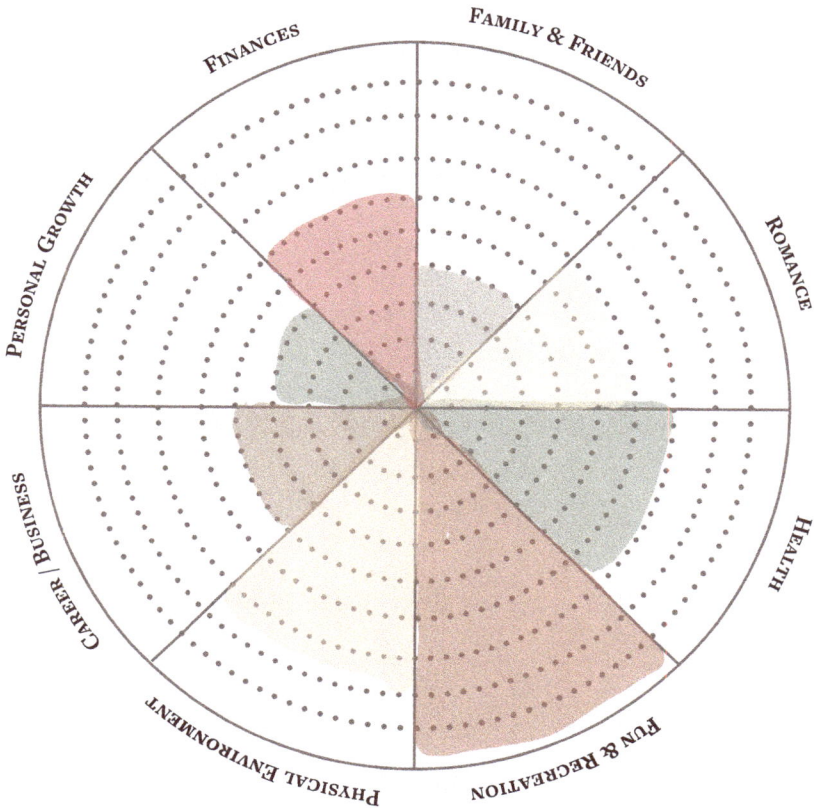

Finances – Stability, savings, debt, and confidence with money.

Health – Physical well-being, fitness, energy, and vitality.

Family & Friends – Connection, support, and time spent with loved ones.

Romance / Significant Other – Love life, intimacy, and partnership quality.

Fun & Recreation – Hobbies, adventure, joy, and relaxation.

Personal Growth – Learning, mindset, spirituality, or self-development.

Physical Environment – Your home, workspace, neighborhood—how supportive and enjoyable they feel.

Are other areas (such as Family & Friends, Personal Growth, or Health) being ignored? Is his entire wheel basically a soccer ball? Does the imbalance occur regularly, or is it just a seasonal phenomenon?

Why It Matters

It's not about the passion for the game — it's about the imbalance. When one identity (fan) overshadows all others (him as a partner, a son, an employee, or a friend), the relationship stops feeling mutual. Over time, this can erode emotional intimacy. If his whole self is only accessible during halftime, where does that leave everything else?

What Partners Usually Do Wrong

- **Become sarcastic:** "Had I known you were married to [insert team name here]...."

- **Withdraw:** You stop trying, stop sharing, stop asking. Pretty soon, you'll stop caring about your relationship.

- **Becoming the Anti-Fan:** You swing so far in the other direction just to balance things out that his only passion becomes tension in your relationship.

These reactions make emotional sense. They're human. But they don't move the relationship forward; they create defensiveness, not change.

What to Negotiate

You're not asking them to change who they are — just to make room for a few other slices of the pie.

Some conversation starters:

"What if Sundays are for the games, and Mondays are for us?"

"Can we each pick one night a week for our own thing, and one night for shared plans?"

"Would you be open to exploring a new hobby that's not soccer, just to shake things up a bit?"

"I'd love for us to do one thing together each month that neither of us has tried before. Let's build shared memories outside of the game."

"Let's each choose one new hobby to explore this season– something that doesn't involve screens or sports."

This isn't about subtraction. It's about adding range — for him, for you, and for the relationship.

The Tool: Life Wheel

Both of you draw the wheel and rate your satisfaction in each section. This makes the dynamic more interactive. Rate each section honestly. Compare notes with curiosity, not accusation.

Check-Ins: Once a month, do a quick pulse check on both your lives outside the relationship and help each other be intentional about your goals.

Ask each other:

"What's something that's bringing you joy lately outside of soccer/ work/Netflix?"

"What's a skill or interest you'd want to explore more if you had time?"

"Is there something we could try together just for fun?"

This isn't therapy or parenting. It's friendship inside your relationship. And remember — following through matters more than the conversation.

How to Use It

1. **Pick a neutral, low-stress time** — not mid-game and NOT right after a fight.

2. **Frame it gently:**

   "I've been thinking about how easy it is to get into ruts — like soccer becoming the only flavor of ice cream we keep buying. Can we brainstorm something new for us to try?"

3. **Ask, don't accuse:** Use curiosity over criticism.

4. **Follow through**: Actually plan or support the non-soccer thing he names. If you name something you want, let him help too. It's a two-way street.

5. **Circle back:** Reflect on how the shift felt a week or two later. "Did you enjoy doing something different?"

Why Use It

Expanding identity increases emotional resilience. When people feel multifaceted, they're better able to regulate stress, stay open to connection, and recover from setbacks.

Psychologists refer to this as "self-complexity theory." Simply put: when all your happiness depends on one thing, a bad day in that area wrecks you. But if you nurture multiple regions, your emotional well-being is more resilient.

Game Changer: If he's not into trying something new for himself, pitch it as a "we" upgrade: "Is there anything we've never done that might bring us a little closer?"

YOUR LIFE WHEEL

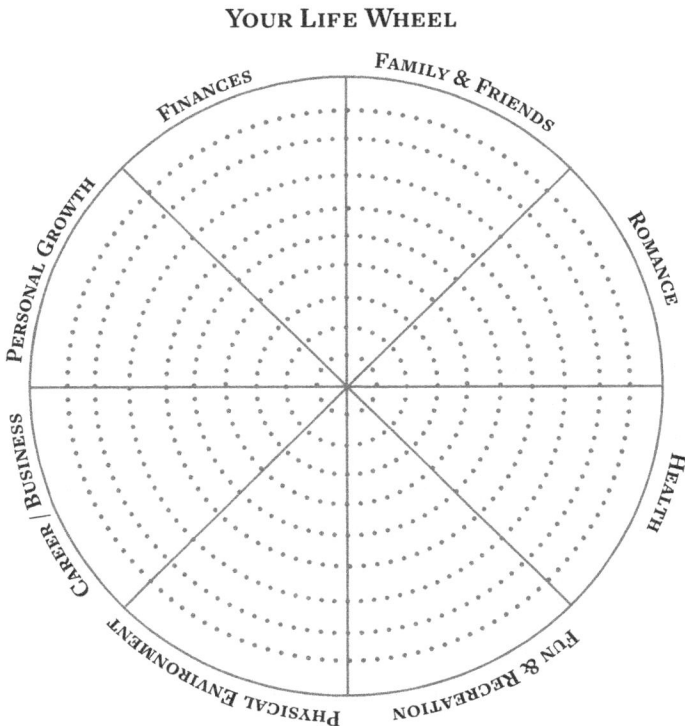

Even if it's something light — like learning how to make sushi or hiking a new trail, taking a cooking class — it signals that the relationship isn't just surviving game season. It's growing through it.

On the next page is a list of alternate hobbies. **The goal isn't to replace the love for soccer** — you're trying to make sure it isn't the *only* passion in life. Before showing your partner the next page, do yourself a favor and black out the hobbies you would hate for him to pick up.

If all else fails, see page 93.

YOUR PARTNER'S LIFE WHEEL
(Let them fill it out).

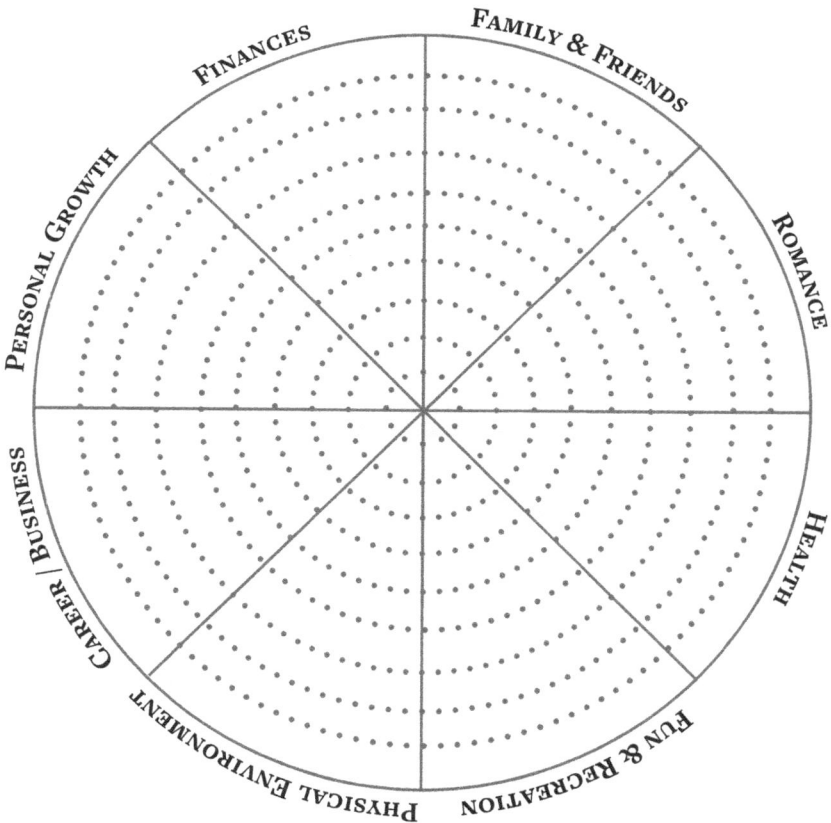

Hobby Menu

Low Cost, Short Time

Soccer (playing)
Weightlifting
Running marathons
Rock climbing
Barbecue smoking/grilling
Axe throwing
E-sports tournaments
Journaling
Movie marathons
Hiking
Cooking new recipes
Yoga
Meditation
Volunteering
Swimming
Magic tricks
Learning a new language

Low Cost, Long Time

Video gaming
Tailgating
Guitar playing
Stand-up comedy
Craft beer brewing
Woodworking
Leatherworking
Archery
Shooting range practice
Coding/programming side projects
Fantasy RPG tabletop games
Gardening
Writing short stories
Chess
Photography
Poker nights
Surfing
Acting/Improv theater
Joining a local sports league

High Cost, Long Time

Car restoration
Martial arts (boxing, jiu-jitsu, Muay Thai)
Homebrewing coffee (geeking out with espresso machines)
Building model airplanes/cars
Hiking and survival training
Scuba diving
Mountain biking
Hunting
Fishing trips
Sailing
DIY home projects
Building a "man cave"
Camping trips
Golf

High Cost, Short Time

Whiskey tasting
Off-roading/ATVs
Drone flying
Collecting sneakers
Collecting watches
Stock trading/crypto investing
Collecting sports memorabilia
Paintball, laser tag, or airsoft
Collecting vinyl records
Horseback riding

Conversations

It's one thing to date someone who talks about soccer. It's another thing to date someone who monologues about soccer. What about you? Your day? Your feelings? This section is for those moments when conversations feel lopsided, dismissive, or like you're talking past each other.

Why It Matters

This isn't about talking *more*. It's about feeling seen, respected, and aligned. When conversations are one-sided, intimacy shrinks and resentment grows. Ensuring that you both feel heard and valued is essential to a sustainable dynamic.

What to Negotiate

Establish a few simple, clear communication agreements that both of you commit to. Not rules, mutual agreements to ensure both people feel heard.

No-Soccer Zones: Dinner, the first 15 minutes after you both get home, or wind-down time. Remind him he is "Out of bounds!" when he breaks the agreement. Agree on these zones together so they feel supportive, not restrictive. Maybe you don't get to complain about your soon-to-be mother-in-law in those zones either.

RED CARD

He shuts down or gets defensive when you try to talk about relationship issues — or worse, accuses you of being "too much" or "always nagging."

YELLOW CARD

He dominates most conversations or redirects every topic back to what he likes.

50

The Pass the Mic Rule: If one person monologues for 5 minutes, the other gets the following 5. No interruptions, no "one more thing." And if he struggles with this, reset together without shaming — some people genuinely lose track of time when they're excited.

What Partners Usually Do Wrong

When you feel shut out, it's easy to default to sarcasm, side comments, or shutting down altogether. Here's how it might look:

COMMUNICATION STYLE	WHAT IT CREATES
PASSIVE	
"It's fine. You don't have to ask about my day. It was boring anyway."	**Unspoken resentment, distance**
PASSIVE-AGGRESSIVE	
"My day was actually nice! Thank you for *not* asking."	**Guilt trips, tension**
AGGRESSIVE	
"You only care about your stupid team!"	**Defensiveness, stonewalling**
ASSERTIVE	
"I've been feeling a little sidelined. Can we carve out some time for us this week?" OR "I miss talking about stuff outside of soccer. Can we take a walk and just catch up?" OR " I know your team is important, but can we also make space for other topics? I want us to share what's going on in both of our lives."	**Openness, teamwork, and emotional safety**

The Tool

Instead of circling the same old "How was your day?", try this quick, balanced ritual:

High: best part of your day

Low: hardest or most draining part

Love: one thing you appreciated about your partner

Laugh: something funny, weird, or playful

GREEN CARD

He loves talking about soccer, but makes space for your stories, ideas, and interests too. He seeks your point of view.

This simple framework prevents conversations from stalling, ensures both voices are heard, and subtly conveys appreciation in the process. It's short enough to do during halftime, but meaningful enough to build a connection beyond box scores and highlight reels.

How to Use It

1. **Pick the right time** — over dinner, during halftime, or at the end of the day.

2. **Keep it short** — 2–3 minutes each. This is about sharing, not storytelling marathons.

3. **Stay curious** — ask one follow-up question to show engagement.

4. **Make it routine** — a nightly ritual, a Sunday wrap-up, or even a halftime tradition.

Why Use It

This tool works best when both partners participate — you're not carrying the whole conversation alone.

● **Built-in balance:** Ensures both partners share and listen equally.

- **Appreciation baked in**: Gratitude boosts relationship satisfaction and counters negativity bias.

- **Emotional range:** Combining High/Low with Love/Laugh prevents check-ins from becoming too heavy or too shallow.

- **Ritual power:** Repeating it builds consistency, so both partners know they'll get a turn to be seen and heard.

Game Changer: If he forgets to ask, start with yours anyway. Curiosity is contagious — when you model openness, it sets the tone for him to follow.

If all else fails, see page 93.

Emotional Regulation

S ome people cheer. Some rage. Some spiral for days. When you love a soccer fan, you might notice that the emotional rollercoaster does not always end with the final whistle. Keep in mind that many cultures do not encourage emotional expression in men. So be careful not to shut down the one escape valve he thinks he has. This is not about judging how emotional he gets — it's about the ripple effects that happen next.

Why It Matters

Not knowing what version of your partner you'll get after every match can create chronic stress in the relationship. Even when you're not engaging with the game, your nervous system is still absorbing the energy. When emotional regulation is missing, things escalate quickly. Trust weakens, affection drops, and everything feels harder than it has to be.

What Partners Usually Do Wrong

Ignoring it and hoping it passes (it doesn't).

Matching his energy to "prove a point" (two wrongs don't make a right).

Walking on eggshells to avoid setting him off.

Assuming it's "just how he is," freezing him in time dismisses the potential each human has for growth.

You can't out-shout someone into being calm. And you shouldn't have to tiptoe around an adult's tantrum. Big feelings are human — but repeating the same explosive reaction without taking responsibility turns it into a problem.

What to Negotiate

"Can we build a wind-down routine after stressful games?" *If he's über masculine, call it a 'tradition.'*

> "If things feel off, can we agree to take 15 minutes apart to cool off before continuing the night together?"

> "If one of us notices that the vibe is wrong, can we pause, reset, and check in? No silent treatment, no simmering tension. Just a quick, honest pulse check so things don't build up."

> "Let's agree that anger or frustration from a match doesn't justify being short, distant, or rude with each other.

> We are still responsible for our words and behaviors."

> "I want to help you reset, but do you need some space to work it out? I just don't want this spilling into other parts of our life."

The goal is to create shared language around emotional waves—so you're not riding them blind. It is easier to resolve something when you can identify what is wrong.

RED CARD

He's emotionally volatile, shuts down, lashes out, or makes you the collateral damage for a game he didn't even play.

GREEN CARD

He gets worked up but cools off quickly and reconnects emotionally.

YELLOW CARD

His mood lingers long after the game, and you're walking on eggshells.

The Tools

Use the Emotion Wheel

Grounding Techniques

Co-Regulation Flow

Imagine your feelings are on a giant color wheel. Each primary color represents the baseline of a specific emotion: love, safe, heavy, fear, anger, and hurt. But just like colors have shades, emotions do too. "Angry" can refer to being frustrated, resentful, vindictive, or furious. "Heavy" can be used to describe feelings of loneliness, disappointment, or hurt. The

IS SEX CO-REGULATING?

It *can* be.

When you're emotionally connected, physically safe, and both of you are showing up with caring affection, sex can absolutely help regulate your nervous systems as a couple. Therapists refer to this as co-regulation, which involves using connection and closeness to shift out of stress and back into a calm state. Touch, breath, and physical intimacy all play a role in that.

But sex isn't automatically co-regulating. It depends on the "why" behind it. Are you using intimacy to reconnect? Or are you avoiding a difficult conversation by calming one person while the other stays shut down? If the emotional ground underneath isn't solid, sex might soothe things temporarily... but the deeper issues still linger.

And as always, sex should not be used to override your own 'no' or his. Co-regulation only works when everyone involved feels safe and willing.

The takeaway? Sex can help regulate emotions — but it works best when it's mutual, respectful, and emotionally attuned. It's a beautiful tool, not a band-aid.

emotion wheel helps you spot the exact feeling you're having instead of just saying "I'm fine" or "I'm mad."

The more specific you can get about what you're feeling, the easier it is to handle it — and not take it out on other people. If you can say, "I'm frustrated because you didn't listen," instead of just blowing up, that's emotional intelligence. It prevents minor problems from escalating into major conflicts.

In relationships, knowing what you're actually feeling helps you communicate instead of shutting down, snapping, or ghosting someone. It also enables you to understand their feelings better. When you can see that someone's not just "angry" but maybe hurt or worried, you start responding with empathy instead of defensiveness.

It's not just about naming feelings. It's about building better relationships, avoiding drama, and handling your emotions like someone who knows what's going on inside.

How to Use It

1. Start with Naming (Emotion Wheel)

Most people did not learn to identify more than five emotions. Keep the wheel handy — even just glancing at it can break the emotional spiral (pun intended).

2. Regulate Yourself First (Grounding)
Breathwork, cold splash, sensory check-in. The goal here is to stabilize your own nervous system first — then reengage. For a

---

HOOLIGANS

In the 1960s, the word "hooligan" was born in England to describe violent fan groups whose passion for their teams spiraled into chaos. Most of that stadium violence is gone — but the emotional wiring behind it still echoes in modern fandom.

For generations, men were taught that passion equals power and that anger is the only masculine emotion. Sports became the one place they could feel everything — loyalty, grief, pride, loss — without judgment. When a game loss leads to mood swings or simmering tension, it's rarely just about soccer. It's about what he's been taught to do with big feelings: channel them, not process them.

In relationships, that matters.

You're not fighting him — you're up against a lifetime of conditioning that taught him strength means suppression, not self-awareness. The goal isn't to dim his passion, it's to help it evolve from explosive to expressive, from reactive to responsive.

If his 'fandom' crosses into threats, physical aggression, or destruction? That's not passion, that's a safety issue. At that point, this isn't about helping him regulate; it's about protecting yourself. Please don't date a hooligan.

---

complete list of suggestions, look at the 'Grounding Techniques' section (page 200).

3. Reconnect (Co-Regulation)

Try: "Want to walk it off?" or "Let's not force a conversation. Just sit with me for a minute." Even a light touch can signal: I'm here. We're okay.

Why Use It

- Naming emotions helps the brain shift from a limbic (reactive) to a prefrontal (reflective) state.

- Grounding calms the nervous system, allowing you to think clearly. The brain takes the reins, not your emotions.

- Co-regulation rebuilds connection and reduces the chance of rupture.

Psychologists refer to this as "affect labeling." Neuroscientists call it a prefrontal override. You can just call it peace.

Game-Changer: You don't need to be perfectly calm or regulated to show up with love. Just be one breath ahead and one choice away from escalation. And if you're always the only one doing the regulating? That tells you something, too. You can model emotional regulation, but it's not your job to manage his emotions for him. If you're constantly the only one doing the work, that's a relationship pattern worth paying attention to.

If all else fails, see page 93.

Suggested Emotion Codebook:

Emotions aren't problems to solve — they're signals. When you know what a feeling might be pointing to, the path forward gets a lot clearer. This guide provides examples of what emotions might need. Every single person will need something slightly different. This guide is not perfect or prescriptive, just a gentle guide to initiate a conversation for a better connection.

Being responsible for your emotions does not mean tolerating harm — or carrying someone else's.

It means recognizing reactions, setting boundaries, and choosing responses, while expecting accountability, effort, and care from the people you're in relationship with.

Responsibility is shared: Recognize reactions, set boundaries, and chooe your response, all while expecting accountability, effort, and care from those you're in relationship with.

EMOTION	WHAT IT MIGHT NEED
Envious	Acknowledgment of comparison fatigue and clarity around expectations, fairness, or contribution.
Vindictive	Validation of the harm and a path toward repair so justice doesn't turn into retaliation.
Impatient	Timelines, concrete expectations, or a plan that restores a sense of movement.
Frustrated	Identification of the actual block and one clear next step to reduce the pressure.
Condescending	Space to feel competent again and a calmer moment to reconnect from equality, not hierarchy.
Controlling	Predictability, shared agreements, and clarity that reduces the fear of things falling apart.
Disgusted	Recognition that a personal value was violated and room to address what felt fundamentally "off."
Violated	Restoration of boundaries, clarity of consent, and reassurance of autonomy going forward.
Hateful	Distance while intensity settles, then a grounded moment to name the deeper wound underneath.
Resentful	Recognition of imbalance, reset of responsibilities, or emotional load that tipped too far for too long.

ANGER

WHAT IT MIGHT NEED

EMOTION		WHAT IT MIGHT NEED
	Catastrophize	Regulation, perspective, and one grounded fact to interrupt spiraling.
	Guarded	Time, consistent predictability, and proof that reopening doesn't rush closeness and lead to overwhelm.
	Jealous	Reassurance of importance, plus clarity about roles and commitments. Space to reflect on unmet needs.
	Pressured	Reduced demands, clearer timelines, and permission to proceed at a sustainable pace.
	Shut down	Quiet space and zero pressure until the body resets.
	Skeptical	More information, consistency, and time to verify trust.
	Suspicious	Transparency and steady behavior that rebuilds trust gradually.
	Tense	Decompression, soothing rhythm, or support in easing the physical load.
	Territorial	Reassurance of security, clear boundaries around roles or space, and calm clarity about what isn't a threat.
FEAR	Timid	Gentle pacing and encouragement to build confidence without being pushed faster than their comfort allows.

	EMOTION	WHAT IT MIGHT NEED
HURT	Abandoned	Reassurance of presence, reliability, and clarity about commitment.
	Alienated	Inclusion, reconnection, or space to voice the distance honestly.
	Betrayed	Honest acknowledgment of the rupture, clarity about what specifically broke trust, and a meaningful path toward repair.
	Bitter	Acknowledgment of the original wound and space to process it.
	Bittersweet	Permission to hold mixed emotions without forcing resolution.
	Disillusioned	Validation of the broken expectation and a grounded reset.
	Disrespected	Boundaries, fairness, and dignity restored.
	Entangled	Clarity, separation of emotions, and grounding to regain perspective.
	Inconsolable	Gentle presence and time — not solutions.
	Isolated	Consistent presence, emotional availability, and an invitation back into closeness rather than a demand for engagement.
	Let down	Repair, acknowledgment, and a plan to prevent repeats.
	Melancholic	Space to feel, soft companionship, or comforting routine.
	Mourning	Ritual, remembrance, or a compassionate witness.
	Raw	Softness, reduced stimulation, and emotional padding.
	Self-blame	Compassion, reframing, and support to challenge distorted responsibility.
	Self-pity	Kindness, validation, and a path out of rumination.
	Sensitive	Gentle tone, patience, and acknowledgment of emotional impact.
	Unwanted	Reassurance, inclusion, and honest conversation about needs.

EMOTION	WHAT IT MIGHT NEED
Accepted	Inclusion, ease, and reassurance that belonging isn't conditional on performance.
Appreciated	Genuine acknowledgment that their specific efforts, presence, or care make a difference.
Aroused	Safety, enthusiasm, and connection that matches the moment.
Closeness	Shared presence and open emotional exchange.
Comforted	Continued warmth and reassurance.
Compassion	Reciprocity and safe connection.
Empowered	Empowerment grows when competence is recognized, and decisions are respected.
Enthusiastic	A shared outlet for joy and momentum.
Playful	Space for spontaneity and lightness without judgement.
Protective	Mutual care and aligned priorities.
Proud	Acknowledgment of growth and room to celebrate without shrinking.
Reassured	Stability, consistency, and follow-through.
Respectful	Reciprocity and boundaries that feel shared.
Tender	Gentleness, warmth, and emotional closeness.
Transparent	Openness reflected back in return.
Unity	Collaboration and prioritizing shared goals.
Valued	Continued appreciation shown in consistent, small ways.
Vulnerable	Safety to stay open without fear of misuse.
Worthy	Reinforced through acceptance, emotional consistency, and recognition of inherent value.
Yearning	Connection, responsiveness, and emotional closeness.

LOVE

EMOTION	WHAT IT MIGHT NEED
Accomplished	Recognition of progress and permission to celebrate.
Capable	Clear parameters, realistic challenges, and space to take initiative.
Decisive	Clear information and freedom to choose confidently.
Determined	Support that aligns with momentum, not resistance.
Equipped	Stability, clarity, and right-sized responsibilities help this feeling settle in.
Focused	Minimal distractions and clear priorities.
Fulfilled	Activities or connections that align with meaning and values.
Grounded	Stability, routine, and sensory regulation.
Harmony	Low conflict and aligned expectations.
Optimistic	Encouragement and a hopeful frame that feels realistic.
Ownership	Ownership is strengthened when roles are defined, decisions carry weight, and follow-through has no interference.
Peaceful	Quiet, comfort, and low stimulation.
Present	Mindfulness, slowing down, and undivided attention.
Resilient	Support that strengthens coping, not pressure to "bounce back."
Satisfaction	Recognition of what's working and space to enjoy it.
Self-assured	Affirmation of competence and autonomy.
Settled	Predictability and assurance that things aren't about to shift suddenly.
Silly	Permission to be lighthearted and playful.

SAFE

Apathetic	Gentle stimulation or meaning-making that sparks even a small interest.
Burdened	Shared load, help with tasks, or a simplified plan outlining priorities.
Burned out	Rest, reduced demands, and support in rebuilding energy — not just endurance.
Deflated	Encouragement, affirmation of effort, and a meaningful win.
Depressed	Steady support, simple structure, tiny doable steps, and compassion. Professional help may be needed.
Disconnected	Slow reconnection to sensations or relationships without pressure to "feel more."
Discouraged	Encouragement, perspective, and a reminder of past resilience.
Embarrassed	Gentle acknowledgment and a reminder that a single moment doesn't define someone.
Empty	A spark of pleasure, curiosity, or purpose to reengage with life in small steps.
Frozen	Warmth, safety, and time for the nervous system to thaw at its own pace.
Guilty	Accountability of mistakes paired with the chance to repair and move forward.
Helpless	Agency restored through small, achievable choices.
Incompetent	Supportive guidance and space to learn without judgment or a reminder of past capability.
Indecisive	Clarified priorities and permission to choose imperfectly.
Indifferent	Gentle curiosity and re-engagement without pressure. A spark meaningful enough to care about again.
Overcompliant	Permission to assert needs, recalibrate boundaries, and reconnect with agency.
Overstimulated	Sensory quiet, lower input, and time to regulate.
Shy	Space to warm up, reassurance that their pace is welcome, and interactions that feel safe rather than spotlighted.
Stressed	Relief from overload, clearer priorities, or reduced expectations.
Stuck	A tiny, do-able first step. Permission to move imperfectly. A sense of direction is enough to break the inertia.
Trapped	Options, autonomy, and a path—any path—forward.
Unqualified	Encouragement, skill-building, and reassurance that competence grows.

HEAVY

Priorities & Schedule

Y ou start noticing that errands, birthdays, and even quality time are being reorganized (or canceled) around matches, fantasy league drafts, or last-minute watch parties. You're not anti-soccer. You're just wondering if there's room for anything else.

Why it matters

Time is how we show people they matter. When your priorities keep falling to the bottom of the list, it's hard not to feel like you do, too. Sometimes it's not intentional — some people genuinely struggle with time management or don't realize how their priorities are being perceived.

What Partners Usually Do Wrong

Keeping quiet and simmering in resentment.

Trying to "win" his time by guilt-tripping or power-playing.

Creating your own separate life out of frustration, not intention.

"You don't have time for me? Fine. I'll make other plans."

This might feel empowering in the moment, but it rarely leads to genuine connection.

What to Negotiate

● **Create a "Game Plan for the Week" Meeting.**

Every Sunday night, sit down for 15–20 minutes to go over both your schedules. This keeps you from becoming calendar strangers.

● **Agree on "Protected Time."**

Choose one or two non-negotiable windows each week that are game-free, screen-free, and focused on connection.

● **Use the Eisenhower Matrix to Map Priorities Together.**

This visual tool helps you both clarify what's urgent, what's important, and what can be sidelined.

● **Come up with a list of "Non-Negotiable Events"**

Have both of you agree to respect special events (birthdays, anniversaries, graduations, World Cup Finals) as sacred events that take precedence over everything except an emergency (work, health, etc.).

● **Have a rotating "Date Night Boss"**

Alternate who plans your quality time each week. This redistributes the energy put into making the relationship "work."

● **Create a "Pre-Commitment Rule"**

Before committing to a game, trip, or event, check in with each other — no automatic "yes" to anything that could interfere with shared plans. The point isn't to police each other — it's to prevent misunderstandings before they start.

The Tool: Eisenhower Matrix for Couples

This tool helps you see where your time and energy are going — and redirect them toward what really matters.

How to Use It

This meeting goes both ways — it's a space for both of you to name what you need, not just negotiate around soccer.

EISENHOWER MATRIX

	URGENT	NOT URGENT
IMPORTANT	**Do It Now!** Example: Game tickets you already committed to, family needs, serious talks.	**Schedule it for Later!** Example: Weekly date night, long-term planning, self-care routines.
NOT IMPORTANT	**Fit it into your spare time** Example: Friend drama, fantasy trades, Reddit debates.	**Let go of these** Example: Mindless scrolling, 12th highlight reel of the week.

1. **Set a recurring Sunday night time.**
   Pair it with wine & snacks or something you both look forward to.

2. **Open your calendars. Go over:**
   Non-negotiables (work, childcare, appointments, birthdays)
   His soccer commitments
   Your needs and plans
   "Couple" time to protect

3. **Use the Eisenhower Matrix.**
   Decide together what needs to happen, what can wait, and what needs to be cut.

4. **Rebalance.**
   If it looks lopsided (read: 5 games, zero quality time), pause and adjust.

5. **End with one fun thing to look forward to together.**
   This shifts the focus from conflict to connection. And leave room for spontaneity — not everything has to be scheduled to count.

Why Use It

- Collaborative planning increases fairness and reduces resentment. It also increases the likelihood of proper execution.

- Visual mapping (like the Matrix) lowers emotional overwhelm and supports shared decision-making.

- Consistent check-ins are a form of preventative maintenance for your relationship.

Couples who plan together tend to fight less and enjoy their time together more. It's not about control — it's about clarity.

Game-Changer: Create a shared digital calendar specifically for relationship-related things. Add reminders and notifications so your phone does the "annoying reminders." Label your date nights, downtime, and "no soccer" windows like you would doctor appointments. The point isn't to be rigid — it's to remind you both what each of you needs to make this relationship optimal.

If all else fails, see page 93.

Date Menu

Long Time, Indoor

Wine or beer making at home

DIY home projects

Practicing music together (guitar/piano/duets)

Taking mixology or cocktail-making classes

Planning and hosting dinner parties

Ballroom dancing

Salsa or Latin dance

Stargazing with a telescope

Trivia nights at the pub

Cooking classes

Playing video games co-op style

Pottery or ceramics

Karaoke nights

Learning a new language

Reading the same book and discussing it

Scrapbooking trips and memories

Painting or drawing nights

Visiting museums or galleries

Long Time, Outdoor

Traveling (local or international)

Attending concerts

Attending comedy shows

DIY home projects

Gardening

Kayaking

Going to dance festivals

Surfing lessons

Paddleboarding

Camping trips

Volunteering together

Exploring farmers' markets

Training for a charity race or fitness event

Short Time, Outdoor

Horseback riding

Ice skating or rollerblading

Taking a yoga class

Cycling

Playing tennis

Hiking trails

Running or jogging

Laser Tag/Paintball

Short Time, Indoor

Wine tasting

Collecting vinyl and listening together

Cooking new recipes

Baking bread or desserts

Meditation practice

Playing board games

Watching classic films

Building puzzles

Social Behavior

If his social life revolves around soccer watch parties, boys-only weekends, or nonstop trash talk with his buddies, it can feel like you're just orbiting his world instead of being part of it. Having friends isn't the issue—how those friendships affect the relationship is.

Why It Matters

Being constantly sidelined — or only included on his terms — can wear down your sense of connection. Relationships need protected time and shared presence. If his friends get all of that and you get what's left, it's only a matter of time before resentment creeps in. But remember, he has social needs too — friendships and group rituals are an integral part of emotional health. The goal isn't to limit that; it's to make sure both of your needs are met.

What Partners Usually Do Wrong

- Ghosting social events altogether without ever explaining why.

- Blowing up after a party instead of setting expectations before.

GREEN CARD

Invites you to social events, but respects when you opt out. Balances friend time with couple time. Stays engaged and supportive even around others.

RED CARD

Pressures or guilt-trips you into attending everything. Mocks you for not loving the game like they do. Becomes someone else around friends (more dismissive, louder, or colder)

⬟ Showing up but emotionally checking out (resentment in disguise).

These are understandable responses, but they don't fix the disconnect.

What to Negotiate

"If I come to a watch party, can we plan a separate date night that week just for uS — not the whole crew?"

"Let's check in before the events: Are we both feeling up for this? What do we each need?"

The Tool: Use the "Anchor + Float" Check-In

Before social events, ask each other:

"What do you need to feel anchored tonight?" (A hand squeeze? Eye contact now and then? A planned check-in halfway through? A pre-agreed exit time?).

"Where can we float a little?" (Let him geek out about the game with his buddies while you catch up with a friend, no pressure to stick together every second).

These check-ins aren't about control — they're about staying aligned before the night even starts. It helps define emotional expectations before the outing begins.

How to Use It

YELLOW CARD

Gets defensive when you ask for more one-on-one time. Constantly prioritizes group plans over relationship commitments. You feel like a background extra at social events.

Before a gathering, check in with: "How can I show up for you tonight?"Discuss what helps each of you feel seen and supported in group settings. You may not have the same social stamina — one of you might thrive in a crowd while the other warms up slowly. That's normal, and it's part of what these check-ins help smooth out.

Agree on signals if one of you starts feeling out of sync (such as eye contact, a hand squeeze, or a code word).

Debrief after: What went well? What felt off? What could shift next time?

Why Use It

Feeling emotionally tethered in social spaces lowers anxiety and defensiveness. It reinforces that you're a team, not two individuals reacting to a crowd. This is co-regulation in public—staying connected, even when the energy around you is loud, distracted, or unpredictable.

Game-Changer: Be mindful of "social auto-pilot." Just because he's always gone out with the guys every Saturday doesn't mean it still works for your relationship now. Normalize checking in about routines instead of blindly continuing them. Relationships evolve. Rituals should, too. Normalize revisiting what still feels good—and what doesn't.

If all else fails, see page 93.

SOCIAL AUTOPILOT

Sometimes, an unconscious momentum can take over one's life. Neither of you stops to ask: Is this still working for us?

Come back to intentionality. Social habits are not the problem. The problem is when they become so automatic that they crowd out the connection, flexibility, or balance in your relationship.

Try: "I know Saturdays have always been guys' night. But can we check in about that — is it still something that works for both of us?"

It's about making space for mutual ownership of your time and energy. And keep your eye on patterns, not one-offs. One busy weekend doesn't define a relationship — but consistent disconnection absolutely does.

Online
Engagement

H e's yelling at a different screen... A tiny screen, arguing with strangers in a comment thread. Online fandom has taken on a life of its own, and it's starting to spill into your real one.

Why It Matters

It's not about being online — it's about being elsewhere. If your partner is constantly "plugged in," it chips away at intimacy, attention, and emotional availability. For some people, scrolling or engaging online is how they decompress. That's fine — as long as it doesn't replace connection. Online interactions can feel surprisingly meaningful for some people — so the goal isn't to take that away, but to make sure it doesn't take over. If online reactions feel unusually intense, it might be about stress or burnout more than whatever's happening on the screen.

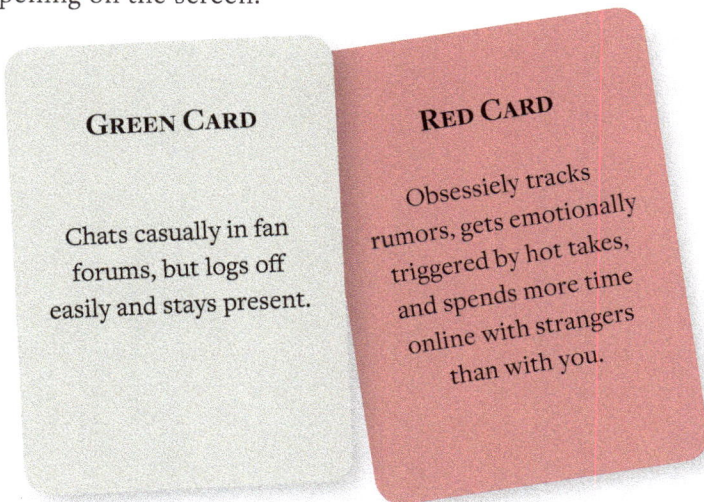

GREEN CARD

Chats casually in fan forums, but logs off easily and stays present.

RED CARD

Obsessiely tracks rumors, gets emotionally triggered by hot takes, and spends more time online with strangers than with you.

What Partners Usually Do Wrong

- Trying to "compete" with his phone for attention.

- Mocking his online drama ("You're fighting with a 14-year-old on Reddit?").

- Silent resentment and checking out yourself. Sulking may be effective in the short run, but it does not build security.

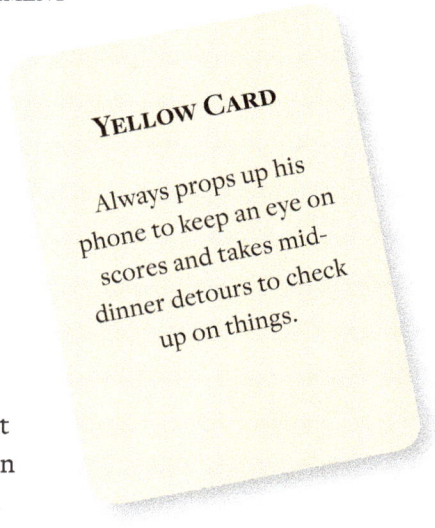

YELLOW CARD

Always props up his phone to keep an eye on scores and takes mid-dinner detours to check up on things.

What to Negotiate

"What if we agreed on no phones during dinner or wind-down time?"

"Let's have one screen-free night a week."

"Can we check in on whether online stuff is affecting our moods?"

The Tool: Digital Check-In

A weekly 2-minute check where each person names what's helping them feel connected — and what's pulling them away (scrolling, group chats, etc.). The check-in works best when each person talks about their own habits instead of calling out the others.

How to Use It

Add it to your "Game Plan for the Week" meeting.

Each of you answers: "What made me feel close to you this week?"

Then: "What distracted me or made me feel distant?"

Keep it short. No blame, just insight.

Why Use It

This tool replaces defensiveness with self-awareness. When we reflect on our own habits, we're more likely to change them — particularly if it's meant to protect connection, rather than enforce control.

Game-Changer: Ask why he's so pulled into online spaces right now — stress, loneliness, or overwhelm often show up as screen time.

Avoid sarcasm when addressing screen time—it almost always leads to defensiveness. Curiosity opens doors. Criticism slams them shut. Remember that several phones allow you to limit screen time on specific applications. It might be worth exploring for both of you.

If all else fails, see page 93.

Gambling & Betting

It can start with a few lighthearted bets, but suddenly the stakes feel emotional, financial, or even relational. Whether it's sports gambling, fantasy leagues, or daily betting apps — when money and emotion collide, things can quickly spiral.

Why It Matters

It's not about the money — it's about trust, transparency, and emotional safety. When gambling becomes compulsive or secretive, it erodes stability and creates an invisible third party in your relationship: risk. "You're not overreacting if something feels off, even if he says it's 'no big deal.'"

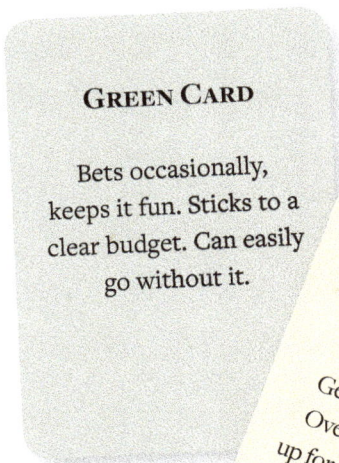

GREEN CARD

Bets occasionally, keeps it fun. Sticks to a clear budget. Can easily go without it.

RED CARD

Treats betting as a main income or an emotional fix. Ignores agreed limits, secretly bets. Hides losses or lies about betting.

YELLOW CARD

Gets moody after losses. Overspends, but "makes up for it later." Gets restless during downtime.

What Partners Usually Do Wrong

Mocking or moralizing: "Why do you waste money on that crap?"

Stonewalling: "Fine, just do what you want — don't expect me to care when you're broke."

Matching the chaos: "If you're going to gamble, I'll blow money on shoes."

These reactions usually come from fear or frustration, not malice — but they still don't move the relationship forward. They often escalate the problem or push it underground. Either way, they don't solve anything.

What to Negotiate

Offer boundaries that are concrete, collaborative, and non-shaming:

Joint betting budget: "Let's each set a monthly budget for personal spending, including bets, so we're on the same page."

Transparency rule: "Can we agree to talk about any bet over $50 before placing it?"

Planning splurges: "Let's check in on finances once a week, just so there are no surprises."

Pause Periods: "Since things got out of hand, can we agree on short breaks from gambling? Just 1 week or 60 days so that we can reset our financial stability? Then we reintroduce betting with smaller increments. I like stability." Breaks aren't punishment — they're reset periods that help the nervous system settle and bring clarity back online.

Ensure that you co-create these as shared safety boundaries, rather than as punishments.

The Tool

Trust Ledger Check-Ins — Therapists use this to help couples repair broken trust without turning it into a trial.

- Be honest about what happened (missed budget, secret bet, emotional fallout).

- Ask: "What would help rebuild trust this week?"

- Follow up next time — no lectures, just accountability. This builds trust through consistent micro-repairs.

How to Use It

Choose a calm moment where you are both capable of finding a solution, not mid-argument or right after a loss. Say: "I want us to feel on the same team when it comes to money — can we set a few ground rules around betting so we both feel secure?"Agree on 1–2 small changes or limitations (e.g., budget, check-in day, emotional support). Follow up next week with: "How did that feel? Do we need to adjust?"

Optional: Use a shared finance or habit tracker to visualize wins.

DATING VS. COMMITTED: WHAT CHANGES

The way you approach betting boundaries should match the depth of your relationship. In dating, you're observing patterns. In long-term commitment, you're protecting shared stability. Either way, if his risk-taking feels like it's taking over your peace, it's worth naming it. Even in dating, you can set boundaries around what you are comfortable with in terms of emotional or financial connection.

Why Use It

Gambling often gives short-term relief from stress or boredom. But it can also spark dopamine-driven impulsivity, which overrides rational thinking. These check-ins re-engage the prefrontal cortex — the part of the brain that supports self-control, planning, and empathy. When trust is rebuilt in small, consistent ways, both partners feel safer and more connected.

Game-Changer: Try using urge surfing as a couple. The next time the impulse to bet arises, say "pause" and go for a 10-minute walk, do a grounding exercise, or watch something funny together.

You can also redirect gambling into a different scenario: get a Scratch Off Activity Book for Couples — that little hit of dopamine from not knowing what's next. The difference? This is a shared thrill, with no fallout — a win-win. You can create your own version of this by compiling things you'd both enjoy. Cut them into different pieces of paper and throw them into a bowl. Whenever his urge to gamble kicks in, have him reach into the bowl (reference Date Menu on page 70 for ideas).

Choose connection over chaos.

This isn't about distraction — it's about giving the brain a different pathway to seek dopamine with a shared connection instead of risk. If gambling becomes compulsive or repeatedly violates agreed-upon boundaries, it may be worth exploring professional help for him or together. You can find extra resources at the end of this book (page 211).

If all else fails, see page 93.

Drinking &
Substances

For many fans, game-day energy includes more than just adrenaline. Some use alcohol, weed, stimulants, or "just one thing to take the edge off" as part of their ritual. The substance itself isn't the problem — it becomes a problem when it negatively affects the relationship.

It may have started out fun. Now every game night somehow ends in tension, mess, or emotional cleanup. And you're left wondering: When did this stop being fun and become a negative pattern?

Why It Matters

You are not responsible for managing someone's altered mood, amped-up reactions, or volatility. If substances make him louder, meaner, shut down, too loose, too intense, or simply emotionally unavailable, that's not "game energy." That's a negative pattern.

Pay attention to the impact, not the ingredient.

- Does he become someone you don't recognize?

- Do you end up managing his emotions or protecting the vibe?

- Do you feel unsafe, dismissed, or invisible when he's under the influence?

- Do arguments only happen when he's using something?

It doesn't matter whether it's beer, edibles, cocaine, "just vaping," or something he insists is no big deal. What matters is how it shows up in the relationship.

Regulated is:

> He knows his limits.
>
> He takes responsibility for his choices.
>
> He can enjoy something without turning into someone else.
>
> He listens when you express discomfort.

Unregulated is:

> You don't know which version of him you're getting.
>
> Substances become the third partner in the relationship.
>
> Game days become cleanup days — emotionally or literally.
>
> Your needs shrink to accommodate his habits.

If the effects spill onto you, that's not a "soccer thing." That's a relationship thing. And it's essential to protect your peace, name what you see, and set boundaries that honor your safety and sanity. If substance use escalates to verbal or physical harm, safety takes priority over negotiation.

What Partners Usually Do Wrong

- **Matching his use:** Now you're both altered, and resolving conflict becomes impossible.

- **Silent resentment:** You say nothing... until you explode at the wrong moment.

- **Trying to control his behavior:** You become the "monitor" instead of the partner.

- **Pretending it's fine:** Meanwhile, your nervous system is screaming.

What to Negotiate

Keep it simple, mutual, and judgment-free:

> "Can we alternate who stays sober or clear-headed at events?"
>
> "Can we agree on a limit for game nights (pick a number of drinks/gummies/etc that feels good to both of us)?"

> ### WORTH A TRY...
>
> **Implement post-game walks** (helps process adrenaline and gives you time to connect)
>
> **Game Night + Aftercare:** Plan a light movie or snack ritual to help regulate if the match gets intense
>
> **Craft a new mocktail recipe** together. Even if it is just alternating between alcoholic and non alcoholic drinks, you might cut the negative ramifications in half.
>
> **Alternate** alcoholic/non-alcoholic drinks or joints/food/water.
>
> **Normalize** saying "I'm stopping here" without feeling pressured.

"One weekend a month, we do dry nights — just to reset."

"If one of us notices things going sideways, can we call a timeout — no defensiveness?"

"Can we integrate more water, food, or breaks into the night?"

"Can we agree to call it a night if one of us notices things going too far? Can we have a code word or signal?"

These agreements are all meant to protect the connection and lower tension. Remember you're his partner, not his mother.

The Tool

Instead of lecturing, use real experiences to spark reflection. Ground your feedback in what actually happened, not in hypotheticals or threats. This avoids shaming and makes the impact harder to deny.

> "Last game night, we ended up arguing and neither of us remembered why. I don't want that to become our normal."

You're inviting growth, not guilt.

How to Use It

1. **Choose a neutral, relaxed time** (not mid-game or mid-drink).

2. **Bring it up using "we" language.**

    "I love our game nights, but sometimes **the energy gets messy.** What if we found a rhythm that felt good for both of us?"

    "Last time we went out, **we ended up arguing in the car** and didn't even remember why. I don't want that to become our routine."

3. **Pick one small change you can try** — no pressure, just test and adjust. Revisit the conversation after a few weeks to check in. Is it working or just annoying?

The following pages are not a diagnostic scale — it's a relationship-impact guide. It's not meant to make you hunt for red flags; it's simply here to **help you name and verbalize patterns if something already feels off to you.**

If it doesn't bother you, it's not a problem!
Don't make up problems because of this book.

	Symptom	What It May Look Like	How It Might Affect the Partner / Relationship
Mild	Slightly louder / more talkative	Loosening up, laughing more, minor inhibition drop	Might feel fun or fine at first — unless it's constant, then it starts to feel like alcohol is a "requirement" for connection.
	Mild forgetfulness	"Wait, what did you say again?"	If it is constant, the partner may feel like significant conversations don't "stick" or matter.
Moderate	Slurred speech	Words blur, difficulty forming thoughts	Starts to feel like you're losing the person you're talking to. Connection fades.
	Poor coordination	Spilling drinks, knocking things over	Can feel embarrassing or childish — may trigger concern in public or with guests.
	Argumentative behavior	Overreacts or becomes easily defensive	A partner might start walking on eggshells, avoiding honest conversations.
	"Buzzed" emotional shifts	From funny to irritated or sad quickly	Partners may start bracing for mood swings, never knowing what to expect.
High	Memory gaps	Doesn't remember parts of the night	Undermines intimacy. A partner may feel isolated, unseen, or emotionally unsafe.
	Emotional outbursts	Yelling, crying, blaming	Creates a high-stress environment, where trust and safety begin to erode.
	Flirting with others/ boundary crossing	Inappropriate jokes or touches	Shatters emotional security; introduces shame, hurt, or jealousy.

	SYMPTOM	WHAT IT MAY LOOK LIKE	HOW IT MIGHT AFFECT THE PARTNER / RELATIONSHIP
EXTREME	Stumbling, vomiting, loss of control	Can't walk straight, passes out, gets sick	Shifts the partner into the caretaker role. Feels more like a babysitter than an equal.
	Aggressive behavior	Breaking things, yelling, scaring others	Introduces fear. Emotional safety is compromised. It could escalate to abuse.
	Blackout	No memory of significant parts of the night	The partner is left holding emotional and logistical pieces — a deep rupture of trust when the partner was not present.
	Dangerous decisions	Driving, picking fights, unsafe sex	Threatens physical and emotional safety — a significant turning point from a healthy to an unhealthy relationship.

Why Use It

Psychologists refer to this as "natural consequence feedback" — it's useful because it avoids moralizing and focuses on observable reality. You're not arguing about what should happen — you're pointing to what did happen.

This method lowers defensiveness and opens the door to co-created change. When people feel seen and respected, they're more likely to reflect and adapt.

Changing drinking culture isn't about control — it's about co-regulation. When couples make mutual decisions about alcohol, they have less conflict and more trust. Why? Because it becomes "our plan," not "your problem."

Game-Changer: Talking alone won't change a substance pattern — rituals and co-regulation give the nervous system something else to seek. If your vibe gets better, the substance use often shifts naturally.

When It's Bigger Than You

You can have the best boundaries, most transparent communication, and calmest energy, but if stimulants are masking something more profound, you can't fix that solo. If your partner shows signs of dependence, secrecy, or emotional volatility around alcohol or drugs, it might be time to bring in backup.

WHY THEY MIGHT DRINK

Sometimes alcohol is covering something else:

Stress Relief
Emotional Avoidance
Boredom or Disconnection
Pressure to be Masculine
Unprocessed Emotions
Old Wounds or Trauma

This doesn't excuse destructive behavior — but it can explain why "just one drink" keeps turning into a pattern.

Knowing the why gives you more clarity on what the real conversation needs to be about. Talk about it **when he's sober**; you are wasting your time arguing with someone under the influence.

Not all substance issues are the same — some are relational patterns, others are clinical concerns. If the behavior starts affecting work, health, safety, or daily functioning, that's when outside help becomes essential. Resources like **Alcoholics Anonymous, Narcotics Anonymous, SMART Recovery**, or a local therapist can help give you both clarity — without shame.

Being supportive doesn't mean you have to figure this out on your own. There is nothing noble or productive in roughing it out alone. **If all else fails, see page 93.**

Financial Habits

When your bank account starts bleeding team colors, it's not just a scarf here or a ticket there. You're beginning to notice surprise expenses, secret packages, and a whole lot of "don't worry about it" when you ask how much the season tickets cost.

Why It Matters

If the spending isn't affecting your peace, safety, or shared plans, there's nothing to fix. Problems are only problems when they're impacting you, not just because they exist.

It's not about what is purchased — it's about feeling safe, respected, and like you're building something together. When money starts disappearing into fandom without clarity or care, it's easy to feel like a bystander in your own financial life.

GREEN CARD

Buys merch/tickets within a budget you both understand. Talks openly about big purchases. Still prioritizes shared expenses.

YELLOW CARD

Avoids money conversations, hides purchases. Says "it was on sale" a lot. Shrugs off future planning.

RED CARD

Overspends regularly, accumulates debt, or lies about costs. Financial stress is creating tension and mistrust. Misses bills or savings goals because of fandom.

SEASON TICKETS EXPLAINED

A season ticket locks in the ritual. There is a unique comfort in knowing their seat is waiting, game after game. His butt is committed — he basically put a ring on it.

Some people thrive on that commitment; others feel weighed down by it. Are season tickets financially savvy? It depends on demand.

Good news:

Season tickets typically cost less per game than purchasing individually.

You can resell games you can't attend. High-demand matches (rivalries, finals, superstar opponents) often sell above face value.

Many clubs offer payment plans, so you're not dropping a lump sum all at once.

And if money ever gets tight, you can often transfer or resell most matches to offset the cost.

Caution:

Profit isn't guaranteed — low-demand games may not resell for face value.

The real financial issue isn't the ticket itself... It's when spending becomes secretive or disconnected from your shared budget.

Season tickets aren't reckless — **secrecy, strain, or skipped bills are**. The real question isn't "Is this irresponsible?" It's:

"Does this fit our life, our budget, and our priorities — without becoming a stressor for either of us?"

Most people don't overspend because they're careless — they do it because money is tied to stress, comfort, identity, or even childhood survival patterns. Everyone brings some kind of money story into adulthood — it's part of identity, not a character flaw. You're not just fixing spending; you're fixing the story underneath it.

What Partners Usually Do Wrong

- "Letting it slide" to avoid sounding controlling

- Making passive digs like "Guess we didn't need groceries this week, huh?"

◆ Going tit-for-tat with your own impulsive purchases.

All of these miss the deeper issue: financial transparency and shared priorities.

What to Negotiate

Money doesn't have to be awkward if the agreements are clear. Try:

> "Let's each have a personal 'fun fund' — no questions asked — as long as it's within our budget."

> "Can we review big purchases together before hitting 'buy'?"

> **DATING VS. COMMITTED: WHAT CHANGES**
>
> The way you handle money talk depends on the stage you're in.
>
> **When you're dating,** you're noticing habits: Does he budget? Is he impulsive? Can he talk about money without shutting down?
>
> **In a long-term relationship,** it's about shared impact: Are his spending choices affecting your plans, savings, or sense of security?
>
> If his financial habits are starting to cost you peace, **it's time to talk.**

"How about we set a merch/tickets budget per season, not per week?" This gives everyone freedom — without secrecy.

The Tool: Use a Shared Financial Dashboard

Whether it's a budgeting app or a simple Google Sheet, shared visibility builds trust. It's not about policing — it's about mutual clarity.

Bonus: Add a "Soccer" category to the budget. It validates the passion and makes it trackable.

How to Use It

1. **Pick a neutral time** — "Game Plan for the Week" meeting. Say something like:
   "I want us both to have fun spending money — but also feel clear and in control of where it goes. Can we set up a way to track our spending together?"

2. **Set three basic categories:** Essentials, Shared Fun, and Personal Fun.

3. **Review together monthly** — make it feel collaborative, not like a performance review.

Why Use It

Avoiding money talk is a predictor of long-term relationship strain. Creating shared visibility + autonomy reduces stress, shame, and confusion. It also protects emotional safety, which is more important than whether or not he gets that third team jersey.

Remember, if you're dating, you're just observing patterns — not merging budgets. In long-term relationships, transparency matters more because decisions affect you both.

Game-Changer: Decide on a **"No Judgment Number"** — a dollar amount each of you can spend freely. For some couples, it is $20, for others it's $200 or $2,000. Don't fixate on the number; it's about building trust and accountability. These conversations should feel like collaboration, not surveillance.

If all else fails, see the next page.

If All Else Fails...

Sometimes, the main issue is beyond the drinking, the obsession, or the yelling at the ref. The problem is a refusal to have a conversation when you try to express how it's affecting you. If you've **calmly** expressed how something is affecting you, more than once, and he still:

- Dismisses you.
- Shrugs it off or turns it into a joke.
- Says "you're making a big deal out of nothing."
- Agrees and says all the right things but never follows through.
- Gets defensive, mocks you, or blames you for "ruining the mood".

Then the issue is most likely his emotional unavailability. Successful relationships aren't perfect — but they are responsive. They are constantly evolving and growing in response to the circumstances that surround them. Every couple will get into arguments, but at the core, there's **respect, openness, and mutual effort**. You don't need perfection — *just effort*. In a good relationship, your needs will be heard, valued, and discussed. If your needs are consistently unheard, dismissed, undervalued, or made to feel irrational, you may need to reconsider what kind of relationship you truly want to be in. Is it worth investing more effort into a one-sided relationship?

Being in a relationship is hard. Being single is hard. But losing yourself is the hardest of all. Though it would be nice to live in a world where things are clear-cut and the correct answer fits all circumstances, we don't. It is a messy gray world out there. There are many legitimate reasons not to leave a one-sided relationship, including timing, logistics, immigration, housing, collateral damage, resources, fear, or simply because the pros outweigh the cons. Sometimes you can't leave right away. That doesn't mean you have to lose yourself.

Choosing your "hard" might mean staying grounded in who you are, even when his energy pulls the room in another direction. It might mean saying no to the drama, even when you know it'll disappoint him. It might mean giving yourself what he doesn't, instead of waiting for him to change.

You can stay — **and still refuse to shrink.**

You can compromise — **without losing your center.**

You can love someone deeply — **and still protect your peace.**

Above all, prioritize your peace. If your relationship is eroding your mental health, compromising your safety, or making you question your worth over and over, there are resources out there to help you leave. If you have a support system, lean on it — they can help you take the next step when you're ready. Love never justifies belittling or mistreatment. The end of this book contains public resources for a variety of situations.

Whether you stay or go, your power isn't in the outcome. It's in the self-respect it takes to make a conscious choice. This isn't about ultimatums or dramatic exits. You're not crazy for wanting more. But no book — especially not this one — can make that decision for you.

If you find that "choosing yourself" is difficult, read *Real Self-Care: A Transformative Program for Redefining Wellness (Crystals, Cleanses, and BubbleBaths Not Included)* by Pooja Lakshmin MD. There are also many books that dive into creating boundaries. Explore them, read them and then re-read them until caring for yourself becomes second nature.

Finding a Therapist

Not knowing what you need yet is a very common place to start. Curiosity is enough of a reason to start therapy. Wanting to feel better than "fine" is a valid reason.

Therapy isn't a mysterious world full of experts who judge you. It's just a conversation with someone who has spent years learning how the mind and emotions work, so you don't have to figure everything out alone. **Going to culinary school doesn't mean you're a bad cook; it simply means you want to learn from the best**. A good therapist doesn't tell you who to be or what to think — they help you understand yourself in a way that feels calmer, clearer, and less heavy.

> **THERAPY**
> Reframe the question from "Do I need therapy?" to **"Could I benefit from therapy?"** Odds are, the answer will always be 'Yes.'

A licensed therapist has already done the training, supervision, ethics work, and real-world practice, so you don't have to wonder, "Am I safe here? Will I get forced into hating everyone? Is this person qualified?" Look for words like Licensed Therapist, LCSW, LMFT, LPC, PsyD, or Psychologist. If you see the word 'licensed,' you're in the correct category. That's a real mental health professional. Note that 'certified' and 'licensed' are not the same thing. Simple filter, no panic.

There is no perfect therapist; you just need one kind, trained human who feels easy to talk to. If the first one isn't the right fit, it's completely normal to try another.

Most people take 3-4 different therapists before it feels right. It doesn't mean something is wrong — it just means you're learning what kind of support will actually work for you.

The truth is: therapy is not about being "broken." It's about having a space where you don't have to hold everything by yourself. You can go because you're ready to process something hard, you want to feel more like yourself, you need clarity, or you're simply curious what it would be like to have someone on your side who really listens. That's enough to get better than "fine".

Skills Based / Practical
Goal: tools + coping strategies

Therapy Type	Main Focus	Best For	How it Feels	Evidence Status
CBT (Cognitive Behavioral Therapy)	Change thoughts + behaviors	Anxiety, depression, habits, overthinking	Structured, practical, homework-based	Gold standard / heavily researched
DBT (Dialectical Behavior Therapy)	Manage strong emotions + impulses	Emotional swings, self-harm urges, relationship intensity	Skills training + coaching style	Gold standard for emotion dysregulation & self-harm
ACT (Acceptance & Commitment Therapy)	Accept feelings, act on values	Anxiety, perfectionism, stress, self perception	Mindfulness + behavior change	Well-researched, now mainstream
SFBT (Solution-Focused Brief Therapy)	Focus on solutions, not problems	Motivation, decision-making, short-term goals	Fast, future-oriented, no deep digging	Well-researched for short-term change
Motivational Interviewing	Increase readiness + motivation for change	Addiction, motivation, decisions, and ambivalence	Collaborative, non-judgmental, self-reflection	Strong evidence in medical + addiction settings

Insight / Self-Understanding
Goal: figure out the 'why' behind patterns

Therapy Type	Main Focus	Best For	How it Feels	Evidence Status
Psychodynamic Therapy	Explore past + patterns	Trauma-related shame, inner conflict	Deep, reflective, insight-based	Strong long-term evidence, harder to study but widely accepted
Humanistic / Person-Centered	Growth, acceptance, emotional support	General mental health, self-esteem, personal clarity	Warm, non-judgmental, client-led dialogue	Well accepted, relationship-focused, foundational in psychology

Relationship / Connection Based
Goal: improve communication + emotional safety

Therapy Type	Main Focus	Best For	How it Feels	Evidence Status
Family Systems / Structural Therapy	Roles, patterns, and generational dynamics — beyond individuals	Family conflict, repeated patterns, codependency, enmeshment/distance	Insight-oriented teamwork, habits, roles, practical adjustments	Research-supported in clinical settings
Attachment-Focused Therapy	Attachment wounds + relationship patterns	Trust issues, abandonment wounds, emotional intimacy	Safe, corrective emotional experience	Strong theoretical base, growing clinical evidence
Couples / Gottman / Systems	Communication + relationship patterns	Conflict, emotional distance, repeated fights	Highly structured, teamwork-based	Research-backed (especially Gottman)

Trauma-Focused / Healing
Goal: process what is stuck in the body + mind

Therapy Type	Main Focus	Best For	How it Feels	Evidence Status
EMDR (Eye Movement Desensitization and Reprocessing)	Reprocess trauma memories	PTSD, abuse, grief, accidents	Eye movements, tones, pulses / not talk-heavy	Gold standard for trauma
Somatic Therapy	Heal through the body	Trauma, anxiety, shutdown, mind-body disconnect	Breathwork, grounding, mind-body awareness	Mixed, some well-researched, others emerging
Trauma-Informed Integrative (paired with other approaches)	Gentle, paced trauma healing using mixed methods	People who need slow, safe trauma work	Therapist adapts to nervous system readiness	Evidence varies, nervous-system resets when methods are blended

IV.
learning the game

The
Basics

Hate the player (or the referee),
NOT the game.

Soccer is referred to as the "beautiful game." Part of what makes that game beautiful is its simplicity. Scoring will rarely ever make it into double digits. Making it easy to follow, every goal is meaningful, every near miss is dramatic, and every match is emotionally charged from start to finish. If you blink at the wrong moment, you could lose the only goal scored in the entire game. So yes, taking your eyes off of it can be stress-inducing for an aficionado.

The Objective

The main objective is to score more goals than the opposing team. All goals have the same value: one! No weird math required. They might tie, or not score at all — this is part of the game. Some cups (like the World Cup) need a definite winner, so they go into penalty shootouts when there isn't a clear winner.

Players

> Each team consists of 11 players, including one goalkeeper. There are four leading positions: goalkeeper, defense, midfielders, and forwards (or strikers). There are also roles: team captain, coach, and referee.

Goalkeeper (GK):

> The last line of defense. Their job is stressful, but straightforward: stop the ball from crossing the line. They will be wearing a different

uniform from their team and gloves. Role: The goalkeeper is the only player allowed to use their hands and arms, but only within their own penalty area. Distribution: The goalkeeper can distribute the ball by throwing, punting, or kicking it.

Defenders

Center Backs (CB): Stay central, block shots, win headers, and organize the back line.

Fullbacks (RB/LB): Play wide, stop wingers, and support attacks. Modern fullbacks run a lot.

Wing Backs (RWB/LWB): A hybrid of defender and winger; they run up and down like they're on a treadmill.

Midfielders

Defensive Midfielder (CDM): Protects the defense, breaks up attacks, and distributes the ball safely.

Central Midfielder (CM): The "engine room"—links defense and attack, often covering the most distance.

Attacking Midfielder (CAM): Creative playmaker; the one threading passes and taking long shots.

Forwards

Wingers (RW/LW): Use speed and skill to stretch defenses, cross the ball, or cut in to shoot.

Striker (ST) / Center Forward (CF): Main goal scorer—often the one celebrated (or blamed) the most.

The Referee

The referee has the most psychologically challenging role in the game. Make the right call? Half the stadium hates them. Make the wrong call? The other half hates them. Back in the day, they played god on the field. The decision on whether a goal would count or not rested solely on the referee. Nowadays, there are a few assistant referees and a VAR (Video Assistant Referee) to help make accurate calls. VAR is only used on close calls for important games because reviewing delays the game. Even so, it is up to the referee's discretion whether an infraction will be a yellow or red card (no, they're not flags), free kicks, direct kicks, or indirect kicks. The pressure never leaves their shoulders; the tools just make the job slightly less impossible.

Referee hand gestures and their meanings:

Direct Free Kick

Indirect Free Kick

Red Card

Yellow Card

Offside

Penalty Kick

REFEREE ROTATIONS

Each match has a fresh set of referees, who rotate from game to game to minimize bias. Before kickoff, you'll see their names flash on the screen: one main ref in the middle, two assistants with flags, and a fourth official juggling substitutions and sideline chaos.

Most fans don't actually remember their names — but it can be fun to make it personal.

If you want to sound like a seasoned fan, try yelling at the screen: "Come on, Anthony — wake up! That was a yellow!" It's oddly satisfying.

Game Changer: Yell it with conviction. It doesn't matter that they received years of training and that you're just pretending. None of us really knows how to call the shots.

Fouls and Misconduct

Direct Free Kick: Awarded for serious fouls like kicking, tripping, or pushing an opponent. It can be kicked directly into the goal.

Indirect Free Kick: Awarded for less severe fouls like dangerous play or goalkeeper violations. The ball must touch another player before scoring a goal.

Penalty Kick: Awarded for fouls committed inside the penalty area.

Yellow Card: Caution for unsporting behavior or persistent infringement of the rules.

Red Card: Ejection from the game for serious foul play, violent conduct, or receiving a second yellow card.

Handball

When a player (excluding the goalkeeper) deliberately handles the ball with their hand or arm. Unintentional Contact: Accidental hand contact is usually not penalized.

Starting and Restarting a Play

Kickoff: The game starts with a kickoff from the center of the pitch. A kickoff also restarts play after a goal.

Throw-In: Awarded when the ball crosses the sideline. The team that did not touch the ball last takes the throw-in.

Goal Kick: Awarded to the defending team when the ball crosses the goal line (but not into the goal) last touched by an attacker.

Corner Kick: Awarded to the attacking team when the ball crosses the goal line last touched by a defender.

Duration of the Game

Standard Match: A standard game consists of two 45-minute halves, separated by a 15-minute halftime break. So in theory, 1 hour and 45 minutes, but it's never that short. Stoppage time will extend it.

Stoppage Time: Additional time added by the referee at the end of each half to make up for time spent on fake (and real) injuries and other stoppages.

Extra Time: In the knockout stages of cups, if the match is tied, two 15-minute halves of additional time may be played.

Penalty Shootout: If still tied after extra time during a championship, a penalty shootout can determine the winner.

Penalty shootouts

Not every tied match turns into a penalty shootout. In most competitions, a tie is just a tie. Shootouts only happen in knockout rounds, when a game can't end in a tie — someone has to advance, and penalties are the sport's dramatic way of forcing a decision.

If the allotted time for the game ends and there is a stalemate, each team selects five players to shoot directly at the goal. It turns into a sudden death between the player and the goalie. This part of the game really tests the goalie's skill at predicting where the player will shoot. Scoring can happen in half a second and requires as much psychological skill as instinct from both parties. At the end of the 10 shots (5 shots per team), whoever has the most goals wins.

Offside Rule

A player can't just park near the goal and wait for a pass. A player is offside if they're closer to the opponent's goal than both the ball and the second-to-last defender at the moment the pass is made — not when they receive it. That timing part is what makes it tricky. The referee has to monitor the interaction of 22 moving players simultaneously, which is why even professionals occasionally make mistakes.

The offside rule is the only truly "complicated" rule in soccer — and even then, the idea behind it is simple: it keeps the game interesting. Without it, attackers could just stand in front of the goal waiting for long passes, and every match would turn into a dull ping-pong of long balls and easy tap-ins. The rule forces movement, teamwork, timing, and creativity — all the things that make soccer look like soccer instead of a playground free-for-all. You have to earn your advantage by timing your run, not by lurking in front of the goalie.

Some offside calls are apparent, others are so close that even replay and digital lines can't settle the argument. That's why people say offside is simple in theory, complicated in practice.

Positioning rule: A player is offside if they are closer to the opponent's goal than both the ball and the second-last defender at the moment the ball is passed to them, unless they're in their own half.

Not offside: A player is onside if they are level with the second-last defender or level with the ball.

If this still feels confusing, that's normal — offside is one of those things that clicks after you've seen it a thousand times, not just read about it.

The easiest way to learn is to watch a few examples on YouTube and use the pause button to freeze the moment the pass is made. Once you see it in slow motion a couple of times, it begins to make sense.

The Field

Standard Dimensions (per FIFA).

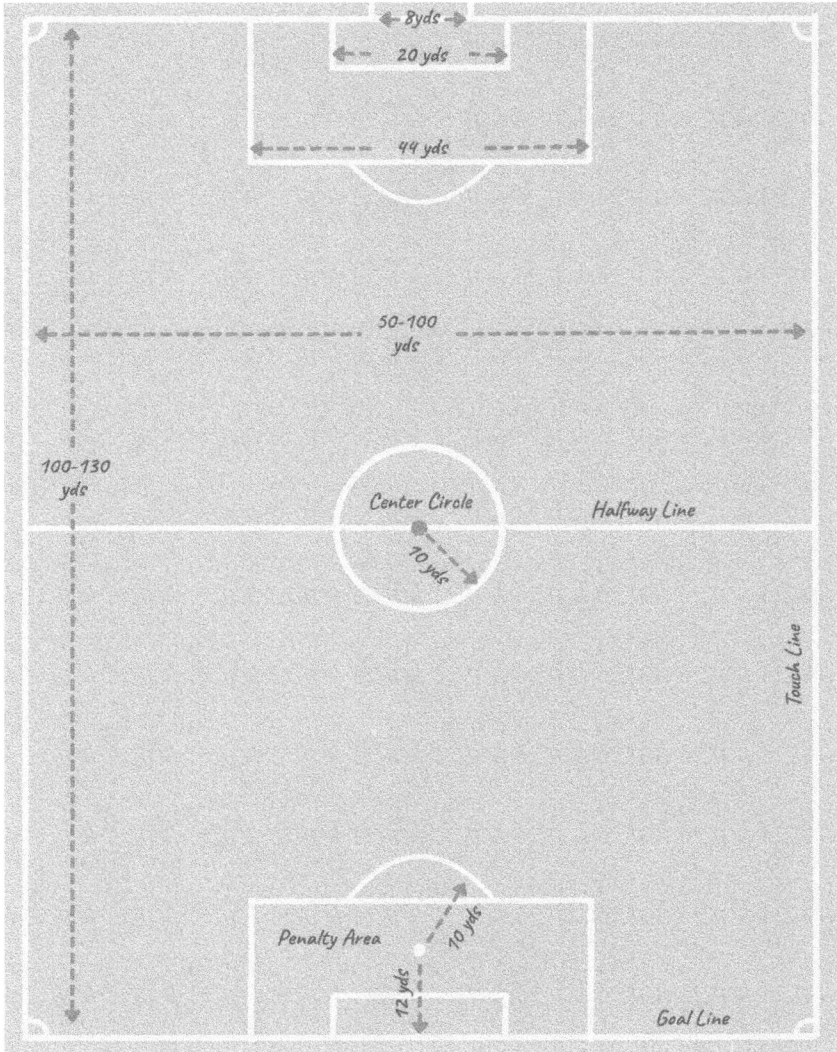

The Players

Most great players are polished from a young age. Most football clubs have an academy where children as young as eight begin their training. Alongside a traditional education, they will learn technical skills, tactics, and the discipline required for the professional game. Clubs benefit by shaping players in their own style of play, nurturing loyalty from the start. Even if players don't join their team, the fact that they have prepared them to compete means they can sell the "rights" of signing a player. Scouts are constantly on the lookout for promising talent, and history is full of stars who entered this system very early—Lionel Messi, for example, joined his academy at just six years old. FIFA rules, however, prevent official international transfers until at least age twelve, ensuring that the very youngest players nurture their skills locally.

As players grow up, they advance through youth levels, facing tougher training and competition with each step. By their mid-to-late teens, the best players advance to reserve or B teams, and the brightest talents break into the first team. This is the stage where potential is met — or fades away. Those who succeed receive professional contracts, offering them the chance to prove themselves on the pitch. The journey is intense, demanding, and often uncertain, but it is the path every professional player walks.

But even the most gifted player cannot win alone. Football is a team sport, and success depends on more than just individual brilliance. Training off the field and shared experiences on it build a chemistry

BECKHAM AND THE LA GALAXY

When David Beckham joined the LA Galaxy in 2007, many believed his superstar talent would instantly transform the club. But even with Beckham's world-class passing and Landon Donovan's leadership, the results were disappointing at first. Injuries, tension, and a lack of chemistry showed that brilliance on paper doesn't guarantee success on the field.

It wasn't until 2011 — four years later — that the Galaxy found its stride. With Beckham fully committed, Donovan anchoring the squad, and new players bringing balance, the team won back-to-back MLS Cups. The lesson was clear: no matter how great a player may be, even two stars cannot win alone. True success comes only when the entire team moves in sync.

that both players and fans can feel. When harmony exists, the team plays as one; when it breaks down, the tension is visible to everyone watching. It is the coach's role to orchestrate this balance, creating not just skilled individuals but a cohesive unit—because they can only achieve greatness through synergy.

Why they Fall and Start Crying

When you see a player tumble to the ground — sometimes due to a misplaced blade of grass — you're watching equal parts strategy and performance. It's called "simulation" (the polite term) or just "flopping." Players do it because convincing a referee of a foul can result in a free kick or even a penalty shot. Referees can't always catch every nuance in real time, so the dramatics help make the case.

But there is an unmentioned element: soccer players run an intense amount. A professional midfielder will cover 7 to 9 miles in a single 90-minute match — more than double what most basketball players run, and at a higher intensity than most NFL players. So it's not always drama when they hit the turf; sometimes it's fatigue, adrenaline, or pure frustration. The tears can be a mix of pain, exhaustion, opportunity, or all of the above.

Men's vs. Women's Soccer

Men's soccer is infamous for flopping. Entire highlight reels are dedicated to grown men writhing on the ground like they were shot, only to spring back up seconds later when the call goes their way. Women's soccer, by contrast, has a reputation for powering through fouls and showing more physical resilience. That's not to say women never flop — but men's games have far higher rates of simulation.

Why the difference? Some argue cultural expectations play a role: men are rewarded for "gaming the system" if it gets results, while women still feel pressure to "prove toughness" in a sport where they're fighting for legitimacy and equal respect. In other words, when a male player flops, it's "gamesmanship." When a female player does so, it risks being perceived as a weakness. So some female players, consciously or not, often choose grit over theatrics. It's not that men are born dramatic and women are born stoic — it's just the culture each league grew up in.

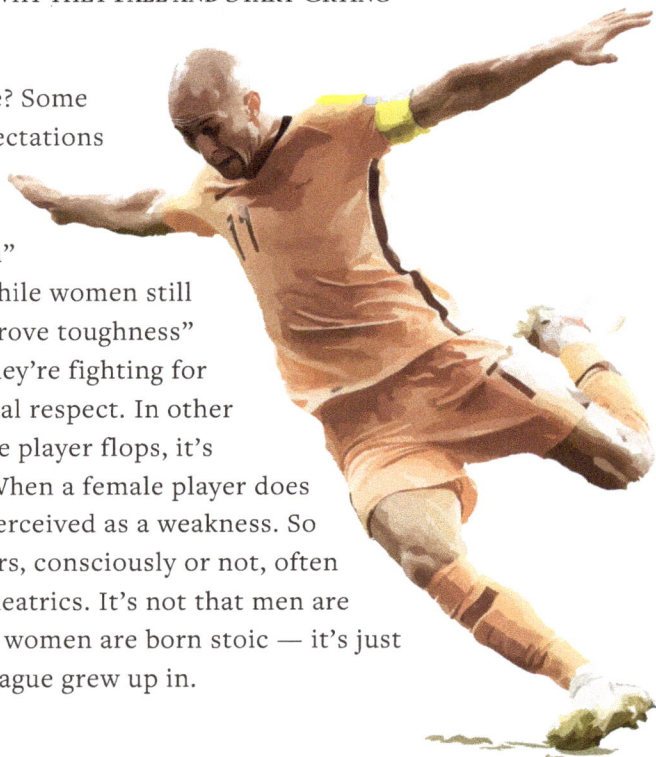

Messi vs. Ronaldo

*The Artist and
the Machine*

Lionel Messi and Cristiano Ronaldo are undoubtedly the two greatest players of this generation — they've spent 15+ years rewriting records, breaking the internet, and dividing the world into two fanbases. They represent polarly different paths to success.

Messi is the quiet genius — a player who makes the impossible look effortless. He grew up in Argentina, joined Barcelona at the age of 13, and became the heartbeat of the club for two decades. He doesn't talk much, he doesn't chase cameras, and he plays like the game is still a childhood joy. People describe him as grace, magic, and flow. His gift feels natural, almost otherworldly. A whole world of soccer data analysts has dedicated their careers to understanding how he shifts the game in a split second. Redetermining the outcome of the game in one fell swoop.

And then you have the machine: Ronaldo. He has the opposite energy — loud, physical, intense, self-made. He wasn't born with Messi's natural ease and talent — he built himself through obsession, discipline, and extreme self-belief. He's a global brand, a sculpted athlete, a walking billboard for ambition. He's not just a player, he's a force. People describe him as powerful, hungry, ambitious, and having a strong work ethic.

If you notice, there is a quiet irony stitched into their shirts. Ronaldo, the man who built himself through obsession and discipline, wears the "lucky" number 7. Messi, the guy born with once-in-a-generation talent, wears the number 10 — a symbol of perfection through mastery. Whether you love Messi's grace or Ronaldo's grind, their careers prove something bigger than soccer: people don't just root for players — they root for the parts of themselves they wish the world would reward.

Messi and Ronaldo deserve more than a chapter. They deserve a whole league!

The magnitude of their recent contracts is greater than what most players could ever imagine. When Ronaldo left Europe for Al Nassr in Saudi Arabia in 2022, reports indicated his total annual earnings (including endorsements) reached around €200 million a year. He wasn't hired just to score goals — it was to redefine an entire league. Not long after, Messi received an even bigger offer from Saudi Arabia's Al Hilal — about €400 million per year, and some sources suggest the total might have approached €1 billion over several years. Had he accepted, it would have been the richest deal in sports history. But Messi said 'No'. Instead of chasing the biggest paycheck, he chose Inter Miami in 2023, where the contract was built differently: a competitive

CONVERSATION STARTER

"Who would you root for if Ronaldo and Messi are playing against each other in the World Cup?"

Follow up: *"Why?"* and *"Which was your favorite goal of his?"*

Let him geek out on his rant and show you highlight reels.

You can learn a lot about someone by who they choose. You're not just asking about a player — you're asking what kind of greatness they admire.

Do they believe in effortless talent or in discipline and self-made power?

salary, significant commercial partnerships, and the option to buy into club ownership.

That ownership clause is everything — it means he could one day purchase a stake in an existing MLS club or bring a brand-new team into the league, like David Beckham did. Beckham's 2007 LA Galaxy deal included the right to buy an expansion team at a set price, which he exercised to create Inter Miami. Messi's contract gives him the same path, potentially following in Beckham's footsteps from global superstar to club owner.

FUN FACT

Canadian female player Christine Sinclair scored 190+ international goals, more than any man in history, but in combined club + international tallies, Ronaldo and Messi are still ahead—mainly because the men's game has offered far more matches and career longevity at the top level.

Feel free to start an argument about this with your partner. It will definitely surprise him. Don't worry, once he Google's it, he'll realize you're right.

These weren't ordinary transfers — they were strategic moves designed to shape the future of football itself. Ronaldo's arrival in Saudi Arabia made the Pro League a global talking point. At the same time, Messi's decision elevated MLS to a cultural phenomenon in the U.S. Both moves spiked ticket sales, TV subscriptions, and merchandise revenue overnight; more importantly, they redistributed the power and attention that Europe has traditionally held in the soccer world. The exodus of these GOATs wasn't about winding down careers; it was about designing the future of the sport worldwide. In that sense, it really does feel like they deserve their own league, because wherever they go, one practically springs up around them.

v.
the global arena

The World Cup

A few things bring the world together: war, the Olympics, and the World Cup.

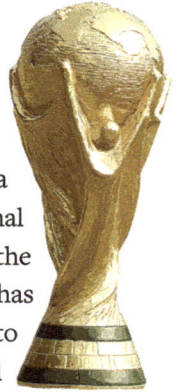

This beautiful and simple game is not simply a game. Despite the politics, rivalries, and occasional international incidents, the World Cup remains the most unifying spectacle on the planet. The 2026 World Cup has expanded the number of participants for the first time from 32 to 48 countries. This is amazing when it comes to improving global representation on the field, but awful for the uninterested partner. There will be 104 total games within 5 weeks. Let that sink in... This means you could have soccer for breakfast, lunch, and dinner every day for the first couple of weeks until the competition narrows down.

Talk with your partner ahead of time and negotiate what is doable for your lifestyle. Even the most devout aficionados cannot be interested in every single game. Negotiate by agreeing to follow a handful of countries

POLITICAL BANS

Russia (2022, 2026 World Cups)
Banned following the invasion of Ukraine. FIFA and UEFA jointly suspended all Russian teams from international competitions.

South Africa (1970–1990)
Out for two decades during apartheid, banned from all FIFA competitions until the political system changed.

Germany & Japan (1950 World Cup)
Excluded in the aftermath of WWII as part of broader postwar sanctions.

throughout the tournament, or cap the number of games he watches per week or day.

During weekends, this can be a perfect opportunity to host soccer marathons with friends, neighbors, or even colleagues. The World Cup, with its four-year occurrence, is an excellent icebreaker for even the most awkward of groups.

And behind it all? The wizard pulling the levers is FIFA — pronounced fee-fah, not phi-pha. More than just a governing body, FIFA is like a diplomatic genius: quietly doing what even the United Nations can't always manage. There are 211 FIFA member associations, compared to 193 United Nations member states. More countries involved, under one game, one schedule,

> ### NERD ALERT!
>
> In 1914, a "Christmas Truce" occurred during World War I, where soldiers from both sides of the battlefield played a friendly game of soccer. They traded cigarettes and sang carols in their respective languages. The next day, both sides proceeded to destroy each other for nearly four more years.
>
> Even though soccer has paused a war, it has also triggered a war in 1969 between El Salvador and Honduras. These matches are little proxy wars for what lies underneath.
>
> Even today, political tensions are noticeable at soccer games. It is palpable throughout the players and crowds — so much so that it penetrates the screens and is palpable from your own couch.

one shared set of rules. Imperfect? Absolutely. But there's something beautiful in that — for ninety minutes, the world feels less divided, because the diplomatic genius behind the curtain made sure the game goes on.

2026 Host Countries

Mexico

Guadalajara
Mexico City
Monterrey

Canada

Toronto
Vancouver

United States

Atlanta
Boston
Dallas
Houston
Kansas City
Los Angeles

Miami
New York/New Jersey
Philadelphia
San Francisco
Seattle

Men's World Cups

Year	Winner	Score/Penalties		Runner-up	Host (final)
2030	_____	____	___	_____	_____
2026	_____	____	___	_____	United States
2022	Argentina	3–3	4–2	France	Qatar
2018	France	4–2		Croatia	Russia
2014	Germany	1–0		Argentina	Brazil
2010	Spain	1–0		Netherlands	South Africa
2006	Italy	1–1	5–3	France	Germany
2002	Brazil	2–0		Germany	Japan
1998	France	3–0		Brazil	France
1994	Brazil	0–0	3–2	Italy	United States
1990	West Germany	1–0		Argentina	Italy
1986	Argentina	3–2		West Germany	Mexico
1982	Italy	3–1		West Germany	Spain
1978	Argentina	3–1		Netherlands	Argentina
1974	West Germany	2–1		Netherlands	West Germany
1970	Brazil	4–1		Italy	Mexico
1966	England	4–2		West Germany	England
1962	Brazil	3–1		Czechoslovakia	Chile
1958	Brazil	5–2		Sweden	Sweden
1954	West Germany	3–2		Hungary	Switzerland
1950	Uruguay	2–1		Brazil	Brazil
1938	Italy	4–2		Hungary	France
1934	Italy	2–1		Czechoslovakia	Italy
1930	Uruguay	4–2		Argentina	Uruguay

Women's World Cups

Year	Winner	Score/Penalties		Runner-up	Host
2027	_____	_____	____	_____	Brazil
2023	Spain	1–0		England	Australia
2019	United States	2–0		Netherlands	France
2015	United States	5–2		Japan	Canada
2011	Japan	2–2	3–1	United States	Germany
2007	Germany	2–0		Brazil	China
2003	Germany	2–1		Sweden	United States
1999	United States	0–0	5–4	China	United States
1995	Norway	2–0		Germany	Sweden
1991	United States	2–1		Norway	China

One ball, two goals, eight billion storylines.

How Hosts Are Chosen

FIFA decides the honor (and headache) of hosting the World Cup. Countries submit detailed bids showcasing their stadiums, infrastructure, security plans, and how they'll handle millions of fans expected to flood in. FIFA's Congress — basically its global parliament of 211 member associations — votes on the bids. It's often as political as it is practical: alliances, lobbying, and even scandals have shaped past decisions. That's why hosting the World Cup isn't just about who can do it — it's also about who can win FIFA's favor.

Future Host Countries

Women's 2027	Men's 2030:	Centennial matches:
Brazil	Morocco	Uruguay
Men's 2034:	Portugal	Argentina
Saudi Arabia	Spain	Paraguay

Notable Countries

This section breaks down the countries that shape the global game — not just who won what, but why they matter. We highlight the trophies that truly move the needle (World Cups, continental titles, historic rivalries), as well as the patterns and passion that define each nation. The goal isn't for you to memorize dates — it's for you to feel the identity of each footballing nation. Every country has a personality, a pressure, a story they keep trying to rewrite.

"Legends" — Who Makes the Cut

> Players who defined an era, changed the sport, or carry deep cultural weight.

> Icons who shaped a nation's football identity.

> May be alive or deceased — legacy doesn't expire.

> Chosen for impact, not convenience or recency.

> NOT every great player who ever lived.

> NOT just the ones with the most stats or awards.

> NOT a Wikipedia dump — this is curated, not encyclopedic.

> The question isn't: "Were they great?"

> It's: "Did they change something — in football, in culture, in narrative?"

"Players to Watch" — What It Is and What It Isn't

> Current or rising players actively shaping the next tournament cycle.

Stars who are still relevant on the field (not just on highlight reels).

A quick cheat sheet: who your partner is yelling about on TV right now.

A mix of veterans and breakouts — not just the most prominent names, but the pivotal ones.

NOT a hall of fame list.

NOT a "best of all time" ranking.

NOT players who are retired, semi-retired, or playing nostalgia minutes in Saudi Arabia or MLS.

***Asterisk Section:** Active players who still matter culturally, emotionally, or competitively — even if they're no longer the future. If these era-shaping names were excluded, football fans would burn the book.

Brazil

One of Brazil's most valuable exports is its iconic players. Most of them began their careers kicking the ball around with other kids in their favelas and competing with neighboring teams. Though it may sound like an idyllic childhood, these were passionate, fierce, and cutthroat competitions. There were no uniforms, no sign-ups, no cleats, no Little League, no programmed tournament, and sometimes no shoes. Just passion-driven competition. This passion runs many generations deep. It hardwires discipline: Training is a way of life, not a box to be checked. The results speak for themselves.

If your country plays against Brazil, brace yourself for a whooping.

History

Brazil is the only country to appear in every single men's World Cup — 22 and counting — and they've conquered five of the trophies (a 23% success rate). Brazil last won a trophy over 20 years ago. This generation of players faces immense pressure to live up to their country's legends and bring home their sixth trophy. They are still icons of the world for holding the record of most trophies won, but Germany and Italy are nipping at their heels. Brazil's football story isn't just about winning; it's about how they win — with rhythm, style, and joy that turns matches into music.

Trophies & Titles

Men's World Cup Wins (5):

Pelé and the rest

Our football comes from the heart;
theirs comes from the mind.

In the beginning, there was Pelé — a teenager from Brazil who made the game feel divine. At just 17, he led Brazil to its first World Cup in 1958, scored a hat trick in the semifinal, and two more in the final. He'd go on to win three World Cups, score over 1,200 career goals, and redefine what greatness looked like long before the word brand entered the sport.

Pelé wasn't just Brazil's hero; he was its heartbeat. His joy, creativity, and humility embodied the rhythm of his country — football not as strategy, but as samba, art, and faith. He played with the kind of freedom that made the world fall in love with the game itself.

Every Brazilian generation since has chased his shadow. Romário, Ronaldo, Ronaldinho, Neymar — brilliant, beloved, and occasionally broken under the weight of comparison. They've each had moments of magic, but none have matched the simplicity of Pelé's glory: winning, smiling, and making it all look effortless.

Brazil may always find new prodigies, but there's still only one man they call O Rei — the King. Yet even legends cast long shadows. For all his brilliance, Pelé faltered where it mattered most — as a father, as a partner, as a man at home. Greatness on the field never guarantees greatness in the quiet places of life. The truest measure isn't how someone performs for the world, but how they show up in the ordinary moments with you. Pay attention to that — that's where real partnership lives.

2002 in Korea & Japan vs. Germany
1994 in the USA vs. Italy
1970 in Mexico vs. Italy
1962 in Chile vs. Czechoslovakia
1958 in Sweden vs. Sweden

Other Titles:

Copa América: 9 (last in 2019)
Confederations Cup: 4

Legends

Pelé — The blueprint. Transcended football, transcended Brazil, transcended earthly limits.

Garrincha — The soul of Brazil's style; unmatched dribbling and pure, joyful unpredictability.

Zico — The creative maestro; technical brilliance and influence that shaped a generation.

Romário — Lethal in the box; a confident finisher who carried Brazil to World Cup glory in '94.

Ronaldinho — Football's magician; creativity, flair, and charisma that changed how the world watched Brazil.

Kaká — Grace in motion; the last pre-Messi/Ronaldo Ballon d'Or.

Rivaldo — The quiet assassin; left foot from heaven.

Cafu — The eternal right-back; relentless energy and leadership across two decades.

Players to Watch

Vinícius Júnior — Brazil's new superstar; electric on the left and the team's most significant threat in transition.

Rodrygo — The reliable finisher who shows up in big moments and turns half-chances into goals.

Marquinhos — The calm in Brazil's backline chaos; competent, steady, and almost boringly reliable in the best possible way.

Bruno Guimarães — The midfield glue; wins the ball, keeps it moving, and gives Brazil balance.

Ederson — An elite shot-stopper with passing range that starts attacks instantly; still one of the best keepers alive.

Endrick — The rising star; powerful, fearless, and already changing games at a young age.

Lucas Beraldo — A composed young defender quickly becoming central to Brazil's new back line.

***Neymar** — Still a superstar; brilliant, polarizing, and unstoppable when healthy.

***Thiago Silva** — Veteran leader and organizer; calm in chaos and aging like a great wine.

Herstory

Women's football in Brazil was banned until 1979 — but resilience has always been part of their game. They have yet to win a World Cup. And still, they dominate South America with eight Copa América Femenina titles and one of football's greatest icons: Marta, six-time FIFA Player of the Year and the sport's all-time leading World Cup scorer. Like the men, Brazil's women built greatness out of grit.

Trophies & Titles

Women's World Cup Wins (0):
Still chasing their first — but always contenders.
Other Titles:
Copa América Femenina: 8 (last in 2022)
Olympic Silver Medals: 2

Legends

Sissi — The original star, Golden Boot winner in 1999, whose creativity put Brazil on the global map.

Pretinha — A pioneer of Brazil's early women's era; technical, versatile, and integral across multiple cycles.

MARTA

Marta grew up in a small town in Brazil where girls weren't supposed to dream of becoming footballers — not because they weren't good enough, but because no one even imagined it could be a life. She imagined it anyway.

Marta didn't just become the best in her world; she pushed the boundaries of what it could be—six FIFA World Player of the Year awards. The most goals ever scored in World Cup history — men or women. Three Olympic silver medals. A career that outlasted entire eras of the sport. But numbers can't define her.

She played with the joy of street football, the precision of a master technician, and the fury of someone who had to fight for every patch of grass she stepped on. If Pelé was samba, Marta was resistance. She didn't just play for Brazil. She played for every girl who was told to sit on the sidelines and watch.

Marta did it all without the money, the stadiums, the infrastructure, or the respect the men were born into. And still, she ended up with the same glory.

She wasn't just the best woman to ever play — she was the blueprint for what women's football could be once the world finally caught up.

Rosana — Reliable, intelligent, and key to Brazil's rise through the 2000s.

Formiga — A groundbreaking icon; unmatched longevity and the tireless midfielder who defined Brazil's identity for over 25 years.

Marta — A generational icon; six-time Best Player in the World and the face of women's football for over a decade.

Cristiane — A prolific scorer with massive tournament impact and iconic moments.

Players to Watch

Debinha — Brazil's most dynamic attacker; slippery in tight spaces and the team's creative spark in big moments.

Ary Borges — Strong, confident midfielder; times her runs well and brings power to Brazil's attack.

Kerolin — Explosive and direct; presses aggressively and drives forward with pace on the right.

Geyse — A high-energy forward; physical, relentless, and always looking to create chaos in the box.

Rafaelle — The defensive leader; calm, experienced, and Brazil's most reliable presence at the back.

Lauren — Rising center-back; composed, athletic, and growing into a critical role for the next cycle.

***Marta** — The greatest to ever do it; elegance, vision, and a global icon in the twilight of an era.

***Formiga** — The eternal warrior; record-breaking longevity and the soul of Brazil's women's football for decades.

***Cristiane** — Clinical and instinctive; a longtime scoring threat and major-tournament standout.

Matchday Menu

Appetizers: Coxinha, pão de queijo, build-your-own Brazilian hot dog bar

Mains: Picanha, farofa, feijoada, cocanha.

Dessert: Brigadeiros, Açaí bowls (store bought or make your own).

Drink: Caipirinha.

Germany

P recision, structure, and discipline form their blueprint, but beneath that efficiency runs a quiet obsession with constant improvement. Their game is defined by control, resilience, and the conviction that order will always prevail over chaos. Other teams play to win; Germany plays to perfection.

History

They've won four World Cups and three European Championships, always finding a way to adapt, rebuild, and return stronger. From Beckenbauer's grace to Neuer's modern revolution in goal, Germany has long been a factory for greatness. But recent tournaments have tested their system — early exits in 2018 and 2022 sparked a national identity crisis. Still, if history proves anything, it's this: never bet against Germany. And the numbers prove it. Germany has reached eight men's World Cup finals and won the trophy four times.

Trophies & Titles

World Cup Finals (won 4):

2014 — won in Brazil vs. Argentina

1990 — won in Italy vs. Argentina

1974 — won in Germany vs. the Netherlands

1954 — won in Switzerland vs. Hungary

Other Titles (Men's):

UEFA Euro: 3 (1972, 1980, 1996)

FIFA Confederations Cup: 1 (2017)

Legends

Franz Beckenbauer — The original sweeper; elegance, authority, and a defining figure in world football.

Gerd Müller — A ruthless finisher; unmatched instinct in the box and a historic goalscoring record.

Lothar Matthäus — The complete midfielder; leadership, longevity, and dominance across eras.

Miroslav Klose — World Cup record scorer; quiet, deadly efficiency on the biggest stage.

Uwe Seeler — The national standard-bearer; consistent, humble, and deeply respected across generations.

Players to Watch

Jamal Musiala — Germany's new creative star; slippery on the ball and capable of breaking open tight matches.

Florian Wirtz — A sharp, intelligent playmaker; finds pockets of space and turns them into real chances.

Joshua Kimmich — The midfield organizer; sets the tempo, wins key duels, and keeps Germany stable.

Antonio Rüdiger — A dominant defender; physical, aggressive, and the emotional anchor of the back line.

Manuel Neuer — The original sweeper-keeper; calm with the ball and still elite at reading danger.

Kai Havertz — A versatile attacker; smart movement and steady finishing in big-game moments.

Jonathan Tah — A strong, composed center-back; reliable in duels and central to Germany's defensive rebuild.

*Thomas Müller — Master of space and timing; still clever and effective, but no longer the future.

*Toni Kroos — Midfield precision and control; a legendary passer approaching the end of an extraordinary career.

*Ilkay Gündogan — Intelligent and composed; a trusted leader entering the final stretch of his career.

Herstory

On the women's side, Germany is just as fierce. They've won two Women's World Cups (2003, 2007) and an astonishing eight UEFA Women's Championships, making them the queens of European football. While newer nations are catching up, Germany remains the benchmark for consistency and professionalism in the women's game.

Trophies & Titles

World Cup Wins (2):
> 2007 in China vs. Brazil
> 2003 in the USA vs. Sweden

Other Titles:
> UEFA Women's Euro: 8 (1989, 1991, 1995, 1997, 2001, 2005, 2009, 2013)
> Olympic Gold: 1 (2016)

Legends

Birgit Prinz — A dominant forward and three-time World Player of the Year; the face of Germany's golden era.

Steffi Jones — A foundational defender and leader; helped shape Germany's rise on and off the field.

Nadine Angerer — World Cup–winning goalkeeper; famous for clutch saves and unmatched composure.

Dzsenifer Marozsán — Elegance personified; visionary playmaker and one of the most gifted technicians in Germany's history.

Silvia Neid — Era-defining leader; key figure in Germany's sustained dominance as both player and coach.

Ariane Hingst — Commanding presence in midfield and defense; integral to multiple championship runs.

Players to Watch

Alexandra Popp — Germany's emotional engine; dominant in the air, relentless in big moments, and the team's competitive heartbeat.

Lena Oberdorf — A modern destroyer; wins everything in midfield and dictates Germany's physical edge.

Jule Brand — Quick, direct winger; fearless on the attack and a key piece of Germany's future.

Klara Bühl — Smooth, technical, and creative; a drift-inside winger who supplies goals and control.

Lea Schüller — A sharp, instinctive striker; finds space well and remains a consistent scoring threat.

Merle Frohms — Calm, reliable goalkeeper; anchors the back line as Germany transitions to its next era.

*Alexandra Popp** — A fierce leader and big-game specialist; still vital, but entering the final stretch.

*Sara Däbritz** — Experienced, technical midfielder; steady influence and trusted in tight matches.

Germany doesn't play for fun — they play for history.

Matchday Menu

Appetizers: Pretzels with mustard.
Main: Bratwurst and sauerkraut.
Dessert: Apple strudel.
Drink: German beer, of course.

Italy

Every match will be dramatic, stylish, a bit chaotic, and fueled by emotion. For Italians, football isn't about possession or statistics — it's about pride, timing, and flair. Their relationship with the sport is as layered as their espresso: smooth, bold, unforgettable. Italian kids grow up playing in narrow streets and crowded piazzas, perfect for developing tight control and defensive grit.

History

The men's team, the Azzurri, is a blend of drama and tragedy. They've won four World Cups, often in unpredictable fashion — when the world doubts them, they win; when they're favored, they implode. After failing to qualify for the 2018 World Cup, they stunned everyone by winning Euro 2020, only to miss the World Cup again in 2022. Italy has qualified for 18 men's World Cups, reaching the finals six times and winning four. Italy's game is defined by tactics, discipline, and a generous dose of theatrical flair (their diving stereotypes originated somewhere).

Trophies & Titles:

Men's World Cup Wins (4):

2006 (in Germany, vs. France — the infamous Zidane headbutt final)

1982 (in Spain, vs. West Germany)

1938 (in France, vs. Hungary)

1934 (in Italy, vs. Czechoslovakia)

Other Titles:

UEFA Euro: 2 (1968, 2020)

Legends

Gianluigi Buffon — The eternal goalkeeper; unmatched longevity and a defining presence for two decades.

Paolo Maldini — Defensive perfection; elegance, discipline, and a standard Italy still measures itself against.

Franco Baresi — The defensive mind of Italian football; intelligence and positioning at a legendary level.

Roberto Baggio — Technical brilliance and emotional weight; the face of Italy's artistry and heartbreak.

Francesco Totti — Rome's king; creativity, loyalty, and a unique blend of power and finesse.

Andrea Pirlo — The regista; effortless control, visionary passing, and a style that became a global influence.

Players to Watch

Gianluigi Donnarumma — Italy's next-generation guardian; huge presence in goal and the team's emotional anchor.

Alessandro Bastoni — A composed, modern center-back; confident on the ball and key to Italy's build-up.

Nicolo Barella — Italy's engine; covers ground, wins duels, and drives attacks with constant energy.

Federico Chiesa — Direct, consequential, and fearless; Italy's most significant threat when he's healthy and running at defenders.

Davide Frattesi — A late-arriving midfielder with brilliant timing; contributes goals and adds urgency from the middle.

*Leonardo Bonucci — The classic Italian defender; sharp positioning and leadership now giving way to younger legs.

*Giorgio Chiellini — A master of the art of defending; still revered, but past his competitive phase.

*Marco Verratti — Once Italy's midfield heartbeat; brilliant in tight spaces, now entering his twilight years.

Herstory

When Serie A Femminile finally turned professional in 2022, it marked the start of Italy's women's football renaissance — or maybe, its first real *naissance*. Once overlooked, the Azzurre are finally earning the attention their talent deserves. They play with the same defensive discipline and emotional flair that defines Italian football, and their growing fan base mirrors the men's: loyal, vocal, and stylish.

They've qualified for five Women's World Cups, with their best finish being the quarterfinals in 1991 and 2019. While they don't dominate like Germany or the U.S., Italian women's football is gaining momentum, thanks in part to the Serie A Femminile finally becoming professional in 2022... About time.

Trophies & Titles

Women's World Cup Wins (0):
Still chasing their first, but getting closer with every cycle.
Other Titles:
UEFA Women's Euro: 0 (Best finish — Runners-up, 1993, 1997)

Legends

Patrizia Panico — Italy's all-time leading scorer; the face of Italian women's football for over a decade.

Carolina Morace — A prolific forward and a pioneer; the first woman to score at a FIFA-sanctioned tournament and a foundational figure in Italy's history.

Melania Gabbiadini — A gifted, consistent attacker; carried Italy's offense through the 2000s with creativity and reliability.

Players to Watch

Manuela Giugliano — Italy's midfield playmaker; brilliant, technical, and central to everything they build.

Cristiana Girelli — Clinical in the box; a veteran forward who delivers in big qualifying and tournament moments.

Arianna Caruso — Strong two-way midfielder; breaks up play and connects the lines with confidence.

Martina Lenzini — Solid and composed at the back; a rising defensive anchor for Italy's next cycle.

Valentina Giacinti — Energetic and direct; presses hard and makes dangerous runs behind defenses.

*****Sara Gama** — Longtime captain and defensive leader; respected on and off the field and a cultural pillar for the women's program.

*****Barbara Bonansea** — Creative, fast, and clutch; a defining attacker of Italy's modern era now approaching the final stage.

Matchday Menu

Appetizers: Caprese skewers or bruschetta.

Main: Pizza.

Dessert: Tiramisu or an Affogato.

Drink: Birra Moretti or Peroni are classics. Aperol spritz (if you're bougie).

USA

America approaches football by renaming it 'soccer'. Just like their start-ups, they are late to the game, underfunded, and determined to disrupt tradition. The country may not have invented it, but it's investing like it plans to own it. The U.S. has turned what was once an afterthought into a multi-billion-dollar experiment in infrastructure, marketing, and star power. All the while, the women already run the show.

Herstory

Ladies first! The U.S. Women's National Team isn't just good — they're legendary. With four World Cup titles, four Olympic gold medals, and a legacy built on dominance and determination, this team is the global standard of excellence. It started with trailblazers like Mia Hamm and Brandi Chastain, who turned women's soccer into a cultural movement. Then came powerhouses like Abby Wambach, whose headers could break nets (and hearts), and Hope Solo, the fearless wall between the posts. Carli Lloyd carried the fire into a new era — scoring a hat trick in a World Cup final — before Alex Morgan and Megan Rapinoe became the faces of modern greatness: equal parts skill, style, and social change.

They haven't just shown up — they've dominated, inspired, and demanded more — equal pay, better conditions, and global respect. And even after their 2023 World Cup exit came earlier than expected, this transition is not a decline. The next generation is already hungry for the next title. If you have the privilege of watching the USA's women's matches, you will witness Herstory in motion.

Trophies & Titles

Women's World Cup Wins (4):

2019 in France vs. the Netherlands

2015 in Canada vs. Japan

1999 in the USA vs. China

1991 in China vs. Norway

Other Titles:

Olympic Gold Medals: 4 (1996, 2004, 2008, 2012)

CONCACAF Championships: 9 (last in 2022)

A NURTURING LEGAL STRUCTURE

Title IX changed the landscape of American soccer long before the world realized what was happening. When the law passed in 1972, schools and colleges were suddenly required to offer equal opportunities for girls and women in sports. Overnight, the country unlocked millions of potential athletes who had been sidelined by tradition. Girls gained something radical for the time: access to fields, coaches, scholarships, and the right to take up space in sports.

Generations of confident, competitive, fiercely skilled women grew up with the same resources, coaching, and legitimacy boys took for granted. By the 1990s, the U.S. had developed the largest pipeline of female players on earth.

But this story isn't a fairy tale.

Two women's leagues folded before the NWSL (National Women's Soccer League) finally took hold in 2013. **It took American culture 40 years to embrace what Title IX had nurtured.** And even then, it survived on grit, low salaries, patchy conditions, and the sheer willpower of players who kept the sport alive. Today, the NWSL is growing, salaries are rising, expansion teams are selling out, and investors who once ignored the women's game are suddenly lining up to get in. It is finally turning into a league worthy of the talent Title IX created.

Legends

Mia Hamm — A global superstar; the face of women's soccer for a generation and a catalyst for the sport's worldwide growth.

Abby Wambach — Ferocious forward and all-time leader in iconic goals; unmatched aerial dominance and big-moment presence.

Michelle Akers — A powerhouse in every sense; fierce, dominant, and one of the greatest midfielders the sport has ever seen.

Kristine Lilly — The iron-woman of international football; unmatched longevity and consistency across decades.

Briana Scurry — Clutch, fearless goalkeeper; her 1999 penalty save became a defining moment in U.S. sports history.

Brandi Chastain — Defensive anchor and cultural lightning rod; her 1999 celebration changed the image of women's sports forever.

Julie Foudy — Midfield leader and cultural architect; helped build the competitive DNA and professionalism of the USWNT.

Carli Lloyd — Big-moment machine; relentless mindset and author of some of the most famous goals in USWNT history.

Alex Morgan — A defining star of the USWNT's golden era; fast, fearless, and the forward who helped turn the program into a global powerhouse.

Megan Rapinoe — Creative, clutch, and culturally seismic; a defining figure of the modern era whose influence reached far beyond the field.

Hope Solo — One of the most gifted goalkeepers the sport has seen; explosive, fearless, and legendary on the field with a complex, polarizing legacy.

Players to Watch

Sophia Smith — Explosive, clinical forward; the new attacking face of the team and a constant scoring threat.

Trinity Rodman — Fast, fearless, and relentless; a two-way winger who changes games on both sides of the ball.

Naomi Girma — Calm, elegant, and elite; already one of the best center-backs in the world and the core of the rebuild.

Jaedyn Shaw — Rising star with a precocious feel for the game; creative, confident, and dangerous between the lines.

Alyssa Thompson — Lightning-fast and fearless; adds pace and unpredictability every time she touches the ball.

Catarina Macario — Smooth, technical, and versatile; a potential midfield game-changer when fully healthy.

Lindsey Horan — Powerful, composed midfielder; dictates tempo and carries the team's competitive edge.

Casey Murphy — Strong, steady goalkeeper; poised to be the U.S.'s long-term No. 1 as the new cycle develops.

*****Alex Morgan** — A modern icon; still influential and impossible to ignore, even as the next wave steps into the spotlight.

*****Becky Sauerbrunn** — Defensive general; calm leadership and years of consistency at the heart of the back line.

History

The U.S. Men's National Team is in its glow-up era. After missing the 2018 World Cup, they advanced to the Round of 16 in 2022, boasting a roster full of youthful energy and rising stars. These guys haven't reached the podium yet, but they are working on it — and the soccer culture in the U.S. is finally catching up. So if your partner's glued to the screen for Team USA, know this: whether it's the women rewriting history or the men chasing new heights, American soccer is having a moment. If you're watching, you're about to become part of it.

Trophies & Titles

Men's World Cup Wins (0):
Still searching for their first.

Other Titles:
CONCACAF Gold Cup: 7 (last in 2021)
CONCACAF Nations League: 2 (2021, 2023)

Legends

Landon Donovan — The face of American soccer's rise; clutch goals and defining World Cup moments.

Clint Dempsey — Fierce, fearless, and relentlessly competitive; a scorer with true edge and swagger.

Tim Howard — The goalkeeper who delivered legendary World Cup performances; calm, heroic, unforgettable. He once made 16 saves in a World Cup match.

Cobi Jones — A foundational figure with unmatched longevity, pace, consistency, and early national team identity.

Claudio Reyna — The midfield conductor; composed, visionary, and central to the U.S. golden early-2000s core.

Players to Watch

Note: Unlike past generations, many of these players were trained and tested in top European Leagues — giving this generation of American talent a much-needed touch of European polish.

Christian Pulisic — The poster boy for American soccer's new era; direct, confident, and the one who turns half-chances into real danger.

Tyler Adams — The midfield enforcer; covers ground, breaks up plays, and sets the team's intensity.

Weston McKennie — A powerful box-to-box presence; wins duels, drives attacks, and thrives in big moments.

Chris Richards — Calm, athletic defender; reads danger early and brings stability to the back line.

Antonee Robinson — A fast, aggressive left-back; pushes forward constantly and gives the U.S. width and pace.

THE GREAT AMERICAN EXPERIMENT

It is not lost on anyone that men's soccer is not America's favorite sport. But Major League Soccer (MLS) is investing like never before. New academies, European-style facilities, and a steady flow of international stars — all part of an ambitious plan to turn potential into legacy.

Teenage prospects are training alongside global icons. Lionel Messi's arrival at Inter Miami has done more than just sell jerseys; it has brought credibility and a wave of investment that's reshaping how American soccer sees itself. MLS clubs are signing European veterans not just to headline, but to mentor. Training fields are filled with a mix of raw energy and world-class experience — an experiment that feels equal parts genius and gamble.

No one is seriously expecting it to surpass the obsession of American football, and maybe not baseball... But maybe basketball? At least hockey? Either way, the U.S. has gone all in. The infrastructure, the marketing, the player development — all of it building toward 2026, when America co-hosts the World Cup. If this generation of players delivers, MLS could explode into its golden age. If not, it risks becoming one of the most expensive "almost" in sports history.

Gio Reyna — Creative and unpredictable; operates between the lines and unlocks defenses with clever passes.

Folarin Balogun — A modern striker with sharp movement; stretches defenses and finishes confidently.

***Tim Ream** — Veteran defender with elite passing; steady, composed, and respected, but past his peak.

***Matt Turner** — Reliable shot-stopper; strong in big moments but transitioning toward a supporting role.

The U.S. may still be learning football's language — but give them time. They tend to master every industry they enter.

Matchday Menu

Appetizers: Buffalo wings.
Main: Burgers and hot dogs.
Dessert: Apple pie.
Drink: Beer, or sparkling booze.

Argentina

In Argentina, football isn't just a sport — it's a national religion. Kids grow up playing papi fútbol (small-sided street games) where flair, grit, and creativity are born in tight, unforgiving spaces. Football here is less about precision and more about feeling. When Argentina wins, the streets turn into an open-air cathedral. When they lose, the country mourns.

History

Out of those streets emerged legends who defined eras: Diego Maradona, the flawed genius whose left foot carried Argentina to glory in 1986, and Lionel Messi, the quiet prodigy who finally delivered the World Cup again in 2022. Between the two of them, they've shaped Argentina's identity as the land of football artists — players who blur the line between game and poetry.

Trophies & Titles

Men's World Cup Wins (3):
2022 in Qatar vs. France
1986 in Mexico vs. West Germany
1978 in Argentina vs. the Netherlands
Other Titles:
Copa América: 15 (last in 2021)
Finalissima: 2

Legends

Diego Maradona — The soul of Argentine football; unmatched genius, iconic moments, and eternal cultural impact.

MARADONA AND MESSI

These two icons bookend decades of obsession, passion, and glory. Diego Maradona embodied Argentina. He was small in stature but overflowing with defiance. He led his country to World Cup glory in 1986, scoring two of the most famous goals in history within minutes of each other: one illegal, known as "the Hand of God", and the other a 60-yard masterpiece that humiliated England. Both of these goals are worth a YouTube search.

He rose from the slums of Buenos Aires to global superstardom, carrying a nation that saw itself in his fire — gifted, flawed, and unbreakable. Maradona made the world notice Argentina by playing with emotion over perfection, and instinct over control. His genius made him a god; his addictions made him human.

His downfall — cocaine use, suspensions, and off-field chaos — only immortalized his myth. In Argentina, they never loved him in spite of his flaws, but because of them. He lived the way he played: passionately, recklessly, unapologetically.

Decades later, Lionel Messi inherited his No. 10 shirt and an impossible legacy. For years, fans argued that he was too quiet, too clean, too modern to ever be "El Diego." Then came 2022 — Messi lifted the World Cup, and Argentina exhaled. The story had come full circle.

Both are proof that in Argentina, football is more than a game: it's a religion with mortal gods.

Lionel Messi — A once-in-a-lifetime talent; one of football's greatest artists, redefining Argentina's identity for nearly two decades.

Gabriel Batistuta — An influential and prolific striker, known for thunderous goals and lasting influence.

Mario Kempes — The 1978 World Cup hero; dynamic, fearless, and Argentina's first global superstar.

Daniel Passarella — World Cup–winning captain; commanding presence and a defining defensive figure.

Fernando Redondo — Elegant and intelligent; a master of control and one of Argentina's finest midfielders.

Players to Watch

Lautaro Martínez — Argentina's leading striker; strong movement, sharp finishing, and essential to the team's attack.

Julián Álvarez — A tireless, versatile forward; links play, presses nonstop, and delivers in tight moments.

Enzo Fernández — A composed, modern midfielder; breaks pressure, keeps possession, and organizes Argentina's tempo.

Alexis Mac Allister — Intelligent and adaptable; connects midfield to attack and makes Argentina more fluid.

Cristian Romero — A fierce, dominant defender; aggressive in duels and central to Argentina's defensive identity.

Rodrigo De Paul — The team's engine; covers ground, protects the stars, and drives transitions with purpose.

Emiliano "Dibu" Martínez — A clutch goalkeeper; strong in the air, confident with the ball, and game-changing in big moments.

*****Lionel Messi** — Argentina's timeless maestro; still decisive, still magical, and entering the final chapters of an extraordinary career.

*****Ángel Di María** — A beloved match-winner; creative, fast, and decisive in major finals, now entering his last stretch.

*****Nicolás Otamendi** — Veteran leader; tenacious, successful, and still reliable, but no longer the long-term future.

Herstory

Women's football in Argentina has been a long fight for recognition. For years, it survived without resources, investment, or respect — but not without passion. Today, the women's team is finally stepping out of the shadows, representing a new generation that plays with pride and purpose. They've qualified for four Women's World Cups, with their best showing being the group stage in 2019.

Trophies & Titles

Women's World Cup Wins (0):

Still waiting for their first — but every year, they get closer.

Other Titles:

Copa América Femenina: 1 (2006)

Legends

Mariela Coronel — A midfield mainstay across generations; steady, tough, and central to Argentina's early competitive identity.

Mariana Larroquette — Clinical, relentless forward who carried Argentina's attack during its formative modern years.

Estefanía Banini — The brightest star of Argentina's modern era; creative, technical, and the player who finally put Argentina on the global map.

Players to Watch

Yamila Rodríguez — Fast, aggressive, and direct; Argentina's most dangerous attacking threat in transition.

Dalila Ippólito — Creative and confident midfielder; connects lines and brings control in tight spaces.

Aldana Cometti — Strong, experienced center-back; anchors the defense with grit and leadership.

Vanina Correa — Veteran goalkeeper who remains crucial; steady hands and big-game composure.

Paulina Gramaglia — Rising young winger; pacey, fearless, and pushing into a bigger national-team role.

*Florencia Bonsegundo — A clutch, emotional leader; her 2019 World Cup moments became part of Argentina's modern identity.

*Aldana Cometti — Veteran presence and defensive anchor; still vital but entering her later years.

Matchday Menu

Appetizer: Empanadas.
Main: Asado.
Dessert: Dulce de leche anything.
Drink: Malbec.

France

Their game is elegant, expressive, and unapologetically proud. When they're good, they're untouchable. When they're bad, they implode in a cinematic fashion. France doesn't just play for victory — they play for legacy.

History

The French are likely to go far in the tournament. The French men's team has become one of the most consistent powerhouses in recent history. Their golden generation, featuring Zidane, Henry, and Vieira, redefined the modern game by blending artistry with athleticism. The new era, led by Kylian Mbappé, carries that same mix of swagger and substance. They've won the tournament twice: once in 1998 (on their home turf defeating Brazil 3–0), and again in 2018 with a ridiculously talented team led by Kylian Mbappé. In 2022, they gave Argentina and Messi a run for their money in one of the wildest matches ever. France isn't just a football team; it's a nation of superstars who know precisely how good they are. Even if they don't win, they will likely go far.

Trophies & Titles

Men's World Cup Wins (2):
2018 in Russia vs. Croatia
1998 in France vs. Brazil
Other Titles (Men's):
UEFA Euro: 2 (1984, 2000)
UEFA Nations League: 1 (2021)

Legends

Zinedine Zidane — A generational playmaker; the artist and enigma; ballet, brains, and the occasional headbutt.

Michel Platini — The original French superstar; three-time Ballon d'Or winner and a dominant creative force.

Thierry Henry — A brilliant, charismatic forward; pace, finesse, and an era of unforgettable goals.

Raymond Kopa — France's early icon; skillful, influential, and foundational to the nation's football identity.

Didier Deschamps — The captain turned world-champion coach; leadership and consistency across eras.

Patrick Vieira — A commanding midfield presence; physical, intelligent, and central to France's golden age.

Players to Watch

Kylian Mbappé — France's global superstar; explosive pace, lethal finishing, and the player every defense fears.

Aurélien Tchouaméni — A commanding, composed midfielder; breaks up play, dictates rhythm, and anchors France's spine.

Antoine Griezmann — The creative connector; smart movement, precise passing, and constant influence between the lines.

Theo Hernández — A dynamic left-back; surges forward with speed and adds real danger on the flank.

Dayot Upamecano — A strong, athletic defender; aggressive in duels and confident bringing the ball out from the back.

Eduardo Camavinga — Versatile and fearless; brings energy, ball-winning, and control wherever he plays.

William Saliba — Calm and consistent; reads the game well and provides stability in high-pressure moments.

*****Olivier Giroud** — France's all-time leading scorer; reliable, respected, and loved, but nearing his last competitive cycle.

*N'Golo Kanté — A beloved midfield force; tireless, humble, and decisive in big tournaments, now in the twilight phase.

Herstory

France's women's team has always been brimming with talent — and drama. They play some of the most technically beautiful football in the world, but internal politics and near-misses have kept them from the very top. Still, with stars like Wendie Renard and Eugénie Le Sommer, France remains one of the most respected and dangerous teams in women's football. As investment in the women's game continues to grow in France, so too does the expectation that Les Bleues will one day lift the trophy.

Trophies & Titles

Women's World Cup Wins (0):
Perennial contenders, still hunting their first star.

Other Titles:
UEFA Women's Euro: 0 (Best finish — Semifinals, 2022)

Legends

Camille Abily — Midfield mastermind; elegant, intelligent, and the creative engine of France's early rise.

Élise Bussaglia — Calm, steady presence; anchored France's midfield with control and consistency for over a decade.

Wendie Renard — Towering defender and global icon; dominant in the air and the symbol of French leadership and longevity.

Louisa Nécib (Cadamuro) — Nicknamed "the female Zidane"; technical brilliance and pure elegance on the ball.

Gaëtane Thiney — Clever, versatile attacker; key figure through France's transition into a global contender.

Players to Watch

Marie-Antoinette Katoto — Lethal No. 9; clinical, physical, and France's most natural goal threat when healthy.

Kadidiatou Diani — Direct, powerful winger; beats defenders with pace and delivers big-tournament goals.

Selma Bacha — Fiery left-back; relentless engine, elite crossing, and a nonstop problem for defenses.

Grace Geyoro — Complete midfielder; reads the game well, drives forward, and stabilizes France's shape.

Sakina Karchaoui — Quick and technical; excellent in buildup and dangerous advancing down the flank.

Sandie Toletti — Smart, tidy midfielder; connects everything and keeps France flowing through transitions.

*__Eugénie Le Sommer__ — France's all-time top scorer; intelligent movement, sharp finishing, and a long-time leader.

*__Amandine Henry__ — Fierce, commanding midfielder; powerhouse presence whose influence defined a whole generation.

Matchday Menu

Appetizers: Whip out that charcuterie board!
Main: Steak frites.
Dessert: Crème brûlée.
Drink: Red wine.

Uruguay

This tiny South American country (tucked between Brazil and Argentina) has strong soccer roots. They've consistently made deep runs in tournaments and punch above their weight. If you get to see Uruguay run across your screen, you'll be watching tradition, passion, and a whole lot of national pride.

History

Uruguay's football story is the oldest epic in the modern game.

They won the very first World Cup in 1930 — then did it again in 1950, shocking Brazil in Rio in what became known as the Maracanazo, one of the sport's most legendary upsets. Despite their size, Uruguay has remained a global force, built on discipline, heart, and unapologetic defiance. Every generation finds a new hero — from Obdulio Varela to Luis Suárez — all cut from the same stubborn cloth.

Trophies & Titles

Men's World Cup Wins (2):
> 1950 in Brazil vs. Brazil
> 1930 in Uruguay vs. Argentina

Other Titles (Men's):
> Copa América: 15 (joint record with Argentina, last in 2011)

Legends

José Nasazzi — Uruguay's early captain and foundational leader; key figure in the nation's first significant era.

Obdulio Varela — The soul of Uruguayan football; legendary captain of the 1950 "Maracanazo."

Juan Alberto Schiaffino — A brilliant, elegant attacker; central to Uruguay's most iconic World Cup triumph.

Enzo Francescoli — "El Príncipe"; stylish, creative, and one of South America's most influential playmakers.

Ladislao Mazurkiewicz — A standout World Cup goalkeeper; quick, steady, and revered across the continent.

Diego Forlán — 2010's Golden Ball winner; technical, intelligent, and the star of Uruguay's modern resurgence.

Luis Suárez — Uruguay's all-time leading scorer; fierce, emotional, and capable of changing any match with pure competitive fire.

Players to Watch

Federico Valverde — Uruguay's all-action midfielder; drives play forward, wins duels, and dictates the team's tempo.

Ronald Araújo — A dominant, athletic defender; aggressive in tackles and the backbone of Uruguay's back line.

Darwin Núñez — A powerful, chaotic striker; stretches defenses, presses relentlessly, and creates danger with sheer force.

Manuel Ugarte — A relentless midfield ball-winner; covers ground quickly and gives Uruguay defensive bite.

Rodrigo Bentancur — Calm and technical; breaks pressure and brings balance when Uruguay builds through the middle.

***Luis Suárez** — Uruguay's all-time leading scorer; fierce, emotional, and still capable of changing a match in moments.

***Edinson Cavani** — A legendary worker and finisher; tireless movement and big-game goals define his legacy.

***Diego Godín** — The ultimate Uruguayan defender; leadership, toughness, and years as the national team's anchor.

Herstory

Uruguay's women's team is still carving out its place in the nation's proud football narrative. Resources are limited, but the passion mirrors the men's — gritty, determined, and defiant. Their journey is one of patience and progress, fueled by a deep cultural love for the game. The next generation looks ready to fight for visibility — and victories. The women's team has yet to qualify for a World Cup, but interest in the team is growing.

Trophies & Titles

Women's World Cup Wins (0):
Yet to qualify for the tournament.

Other Titles (Women's):
Copa América Femenina: Best finish — Fourth Place (2006, 2018)

Legends

Adriana Castillo — One of Uruguay's early standouts; a consistent attacking presence who helped lift the program through its foundational years.

Laura Felipe — A long-serving defender with leadership and resilience; a stabilizing presence during Uruguay's most competitive cycles.

Players to Watch

Esperanza Pizarro — Dynamic young forward; aggressive, fast, and Uruguay's clearest attacking spark moving into the next cycle.

Belén Aquino — Creative, confident midfielder; drives Uruguay forward and brings much-needed flair and control.

Daiana Farías — Strong, composed defender; anchors the back line with maturity beyond her age.

Sabrina Soravilla — Tireless midfielder; breaks up play, presses well, and gives Uruguay structure.

Romina Núñez — Versatile attacker; clever movement and a growing influence in Uruguay's front line.

*Carolina Birizamberri — Hard-working forward and longtime leader; reliable scorer entering the final stretch of her career.

*Lorena González — Veteran defender with years of service; steady presence and mentor for the next generation.

Matchday Menu

Appetizers: Chorizo.
Main: Asado.
Dessert: Flan.
Drink: Medio y medio — half wine, half champagne.

Spain

S pain plays football the way a matador moves — fluid, graceful, and fearless under pressure. Their style is deliberate, their rhythm hypnotic, and their confidence unshakable. Spain's game is built on precision and patience — an art form where control is the ultimate display of dominance. When they're at their best, they don't just defeat opponents; they disarm them.

History

For decades, Spain was football's great paradox — all flair, no finish. That changed with the "Golden Generation" of 2008–2012. Led by Xavi, Iniesta, and Casillas, Spain mastered tiki-taka, a style of quick, controlled passing that left rivals dizzy and defenses helpless. In that era, they won everything — Euro 2008, the 2010 World Cup, and Euro 2012 — playing with the patience of artists and the precision of surgeons.

Since then, the nation has rebuilt with familiar poise: calm, confident, always dangerous. Whether dictating tempo or striking on the counter, Spain still plays like a matador in complete control — poised, calculating, and ready to deliver the final blow in elegant style.

Trophies & Titles

Men's World Cup Wins (1):
2010 in South Africa vs. the Netherlands
Other Titles:
UEFA Euro: 4 (1964, 2008, 2012, 2024)
UEFA Nations League: 2023

Legends

Xavi Hernández — The blueprint of Spanish football; unmatched vision and the mind behind tiki-taka's rise.

Andrés Iniesta — Spain's quiet genius; iconic goals and effortless control in the most significant moments.

Iker Casillas — The captain and shot-stopping hero; calm presence and clutch saves across generations.

Carles Puyol — A fierce leader in defense; heart, grit, and unquestioned authority at the back.

Sergio Ramos — A commanding, charismatic defender; big goals, great moments, and massive cultural influence.

David Villa — Spain's all-time top scorer; quick, clinical, and essential to their golden run.

Players to Watch

Rodri — Spain's midfield anchor; calm under pressure and the player who controls their entire rhythm.

Lamine Yamal — A generational young talent; fearless on the wing and already creating chances at the elite level.

Pedri — Smooth, intelligent, and technical; connects everything and gives Spain its signature flow.

Martín Zubimendi — A disciplined holding midfielder; positionally intelligent, press-resistant, and balanced when games get chaotic.

Dani Olmo — A versatile attacking presence; sharp between the lines, decisive in tight spaces, and often the catalyst for a breakthrough.

Mikel Oyarzabal — A composed finisher and reliable leader; smart movement, steady decision-making, and a delivers in big moments.

Nico Williams — A dynamic winger; explosive pace, fearless dribbling, and a constant threat stretching defenses wide.

*Sergio Busquets — The master of control; defined Spain's midfield for over a decade and remains culturally central.

*Jordi Alba** — Spain's long-time left-back; quick, creative, and a key part of their golden era identity.

Herstory

Spain's women's team is the newest powerhouse in global football. After years of being overlooked, they stormed into the spotlight with skill and a new kind of authority — culminating in their first World Cup win in 2023. This new generation is bold, outspoken, and unapologetic about demanding respect. Their rise marks the start of a new era — one that may even outshine the men's golden years.

Trophies & Titles

Woman's World Cup Wins (1):

2023 in Australia & New Zealand vs. England

Other Titles:

UEFA Women's Euro: 0 (Best finish — Semifinals, 1997 and 2022)

UEFA Women's Nations League: 2 (2024, 2025)

Legends

Verónica (Vero) Boquete — Spain's early global star; creative, relentless, and the leader who pushed Spanish women's football onto the world stage.

Jenni Hermoso — Elegant, intelligent, and Spain's all-time top scorer; a defining figure of the modern era and a master of space and timing.

Alexia Putellas — A two-time Ballon d'Or winner and the face of Spain's football revolution; vision, control, and leadership wrapped in one generational player.

Players to Watch

Aitana Bonmatí — The engine and the brain; tempo-setter, line-breaker, and often the best midfielder on any pitch she steps onto.

Olga Carmona — Composed, clutch full-back; World Cup–winning goal scorer and vital in both defense and buildup.

Salma Paralluelo — Spain's unstoppable weapon in transition; pace, power, and game-changing goals at an absurdly young age.

Cata Coll — Calm, commanding goalkeeper; stepped up in the most significant moments and seized the No. 1 shirt with authority.

Mapi León — One of the world's best defenders; elite positioning, strong in duels, and crucial in Spain's possession game.

Patri Guijarro — Press-resistant, thoughtful, and balanced; links everything in midfield and excels in high-stakes matches.

*Alexia Putellas — Spain's iconic playmaker; a modern superstar whose influence on the national team and global women's football still echoes every time she steps on the pitch.

*Irene Paredes — Veteran defender and long-time leader; steady, respected, and entering her twilight with class.

*Mariona Caldentey — Technical, creative forward with years of influence; still sharp but transitioning out of her peak phase.

Matchday Menu

Tapas: Patatas bravas and jamón ibérico.
Main: Paella.
Dessert: Churros with thick chocolate.
Drink: Sangria and Rioja.

England

The country's relationship with the game is part pride, part heartbreak, and absolutely dramatic. Football here isn't a hobby; it's a heritage. Every generation believes this will finally be the one to "bring it home," and with every heartbreak the nation mourns, but their devotion never fades. England's fans are loyal and loud, though slightly traumatized by penalty shootouts.

History

The men's team lives in the shadow of 1966 — their one and only World Cup victory, won on home soil. Every four years since then, the country rallies into a chant: "This is our year," and "It's coming home" echoes across pubs, parks, and living rooms. Then comes the emotional rollercoaster. They've come close — semifinal in 2018, a Euro final in 2021 — but the pattern remains familiar: hope, chaos, collapse, repeat. The curse isn't that they lose; it's that they care so much every single time.

Just be warned: If they lose on penalties, you can expect much pacing, deep sighs, and a conspiracy theory or two. If they win again, the country will probably shut down and celebrate for a week.

Trophies & Titles

World Cup Wins (1):
  1966 in England vs. West Germany
Other Titles:
  UEFA Euro: 0 (Runners-up in 2020)

Legends

Bobby Charlton — The face of England's 1966 triumph; powerful shooting, leadership, and generational influence.

Wayne Rooney — A fierce, gifted forward; all-time top scorer and a defining star of the modern era.

David Beckham — A cultural icon; world-class delivery, free kicks, and global impact beyond the pitch.

Steven Gerrard — Combative and inspirational; long-range goals and big moments defined his style.

THE ENGLISH PARADOX

The English are credited with popularizing football (soccer). And each season, they pour billions into the English Premier League — the richest, most-watched league in the world. However, most of that investment goes to foreign stars, rather than English ones. The Irony? The country that created the modern game has struggled for most of a century to win its second World Cup title... You know Brits and their titles.

England's heartbreak almost turned lethal when David Beckham was red-carded in 1998 for a petty retaliation. As their best player, he was blamed relentlessly for the loss. For months, tabloids crucified Beckham, effigies burned, fans sent death threats, and stadiums booed. These frustrated conquerors lashed out and blamed the poor chap for their inability to dominate the world (cup).

But in time, with discipline and relentless determination, Beckham rebuilt himself and became a point of pride for the same nation that once vilified him.

He was knighted for his contributions to football and charity in 2025. Sir David Beckham received the ultimate redemption: England forgave its prodigal son and honored the man who rose from national scapegoat to national treasure.

P.S.- Sir Beckham retired as a soccer player in 2013 and now co-owns the MLS Inter-Miami Football Club.

Frank Lampard — A prolific midfielder; precise finishing and unmatched goal-scoring instincts from deep.

Paul Scholes — A technical mastermind; passing range, intelligence, and quiet brilliance in midfield.

Peter Shilton — England's most-capped player; steady, consistent, and a benchmark for longevity.

Players to Watch

Harry Kane — England's all-time top scorer; clinical finishing, smart movement, and the anchor of their attack.

Jude Bellingham — A complete modern midfielder; influential, creative, and already England's heartbeat.

Bukayo Saka — Consistent and composed; attacks with pace, intelligence, and end product on the right.

Declan Rice — England's midfield shield; wins duels, covers space, and brings control under pressure.

Phil Foden — Technical and fluid; drifts into pockets and creates chances with quick feet and vision.

Cole Palmer — Calm and confident; finds clever angles and adds real creativity around the box.

John Stones — England's most elegant defender; reads play well and builds attacks from the back.

*****Jordan Henderson** — Longtime midfield leader; experienced and respected, but no longer central to England's future.

*****Kyle Walker** — One of the fastest defenders of his era; reliable, seasoned, and approaching his final competitive years.

Herstory

The Lionesses have become everything the men's team dreams of being — united, confident, and victorious. England's women made history by winning the 2022 UEFA Women's Euro on home soil, inspiring a generation and proving the power of investment and belief. Their connection with fans and each other is what could make them unstoppable. "It's coming home" now applies more to the women's team than the men.

Trophies & Titles

Women's World Cup Wins (0):
Came heartbreakingly close in 2023, losing to Spain in the final.
Other Titles:
UEFA Women's Euro: 1 (2022)

Legends

Kelly Smith — England's first true superstar; fearless, creative, and the player who dragged the program into a new era.

Fara Williams — The steady heartbeat of multiple generations; England's most-capped player and the midfield compass for over a decade.

Casey Stoney — A defining leader who helped professionalize the Lionesses; strict, disciplined, and culturally foundational.

Steph Houghton — The face of England's modern rise; commanding, composed, and the captain who reshaped expectations.

Karen Carney — Technical, clever, and influential across eras; a bridge between England's beginnings and its breakthrough years.

Players to Watch

Lauren James — England's rising superstar; unpredictable, powerful, and capable of changing games with one touch.

Chloe Kelly — Direct and energetic; famous for clutch moments and a constant threat from vast areas.

Alessia Russo — Smart, composed striker; links play well and steps up in big tournaments.

Ella Toone — Confident, technical midfielder; finds pockets and delivers goals from late runs.

Georgia Stanway — A fierce all-rounder; covers ground, wins duels, and hits rockets from distance.

Keira Walsh — The midfield compass; calm under pressure, and the player who makes England's possession game work.

Millie Bright — Strong, vocal defender; organizes the back line and dominates physically.

Mary Earps — One of the world's best keepers; sharp reflexes and big-moment composure.

*Lucy Bronze — One of the best full-backs of her generation; powerful, experienced, and still vital but approaching her twilight.

*Jill Scott — The heart of England's midfield for years; towering presence, massive personality, and a cultural icon of the Lionesses era.

Matchday Menu

Starter: Crisps (salt & vinegar).
Main: Fish and chips — comfort food for a heartbreak.
Dessert: Sticky toffee pudding — for when penalties go wrong.
Drink: A pint, any pint. Hope on tap.
Suggested drinking game: During penalty shootouts, take a shot every time they don't.

Japan

J apan is one of the most disciplined and technically sharp teams in the tournament. Japan may not be the loudest team on the field, but they're often the smoothest, known for their precise passing, incredible stamina, and team-first mentality. Japan doesn't overwhelm opponents; it outthinks them. Football here feels less like chaos and more like choreography — clean, controlled, and quietly beautiful.

Herstory

Japan's women's team, Nadeshiko Japan, is proof that grace can be just as lethal as power. In 2011, they made history by becoming the first Asian nation — men's or women's — to win a World Cup, defeating the powerhouse United States in a final that stunned the world. That victory carried far more weight than sport. Just months earlier, Japan had been ransacked by the Tōhoku earthquake and tsunami. Their improbable run became a symbol of national healing — a story of unity, endurance, and hope when the country needed it most.

They reached the final again in 2015, proving their brilliance was no miracle but mastery. Their game is defined by patience in possession, surgical finishing, and unshakable composure under pressure. Whether dismantling flashier teams or quietly dictating tempo, Japan reminds the world that beauty and precision can still conquer giants.:

Trophies & Titles

Women's World Cup Wins (1):
2011 in Germany vs. the USA

Other Titles:
AFC Women's Asian Cup: 2 (2014, 2018)
Olympic Silver Medal: 1 (2012)

Legends

Homare Sawa — Japan's most outstanding player, World Cup MVP, and the leader who defined the golden era.

Aya Miyama — Elegant midfielder with world-class delivery; a creative heartbeat of Japan's most successful teams.

Saki Kumagai — Ice-cold leader; Champions League winner and the defensive anchor of Japan's global rise.

Nahomi Kawasumi — Clever, technical winger; key creator in Japan's 2011 World Cup triumph.

Shinobu Ohno — Smooth and intelligent attacker; helped carry Japan's attacking identity across multiple cycles.

Players to Watch

Hinata Miyazawa — Sharp, goal-scoring midfielder; times her runs perfectly and thrives in transition.

Aoba Fujino — Rising young star; fearless, technical, and already a creative spark on the wing.

Yui Hasegawa — Japan's midfield brain; tidy, composed, and the player who sets their tempo.

Hana Takahashi — Calm, reliable defender; strong in duels and growing into a leadership role.

Jun Endo — Technical winger with excellent vision; stretches play and creates clean chances out wide.

Ayaka Yamashita — Confident, agile goalkeeper; excellent shot-stopper and crucial for Japan's build-up play.

*Mana Iwabuchi — Creative, energetic, and technically gifted; long a fan favorite and a bridge between eras.

*Yuika Sugasawa** — Strong, composed striker; reliable scoring threat entering her twilight years.

History

On the men's side, Japan has become a consistent presence in the World Cup. They've qualified for every World Cup since 1998 and reached the Round of 16 several times — most recently in 2022, when they shocked everyone by beating both Germany and Spain in the group stage. Yes, Japan pulled that off. They eventually lost to Croatia on penalties, but not without earning worldwide respect. In recent years, Japan has gained a reputation for precision passing, tireless pressing, and a team-first mentality that has made it one of the most respected squads in Asia.

Trophies & Titles

Men's World Cup Wins (0):
Consistent qualifiers, still chasing the quarterfinal breakthrough.
Other Titles:
AFC Asian Cup: 4 (1992, 2000, 2004, 2011)

Legends

Hidetoshi Nakata — Japan's global breakthrough star; stylish, influential, and foundational to the nation's footballing rise.

Kunishige Kamamoto — Prolific and dominant; Japan's early scoring icon and a giant of Asian football history.

Shunsuke Nakamura — The free-kick master; elegant technique and one of Japan's most gifted playmakers.

Keisuke Honda — Confident and decisive; World Cup heroics and big-game goals made him a national symbol.

Shinji Kagawa — Creative and intelligent; the European-era star who brought Japanese football to a higher stage.

Players to Watch

Kaoru Mitoma — Japan's standout winger; sharp dribbling, quick acceleration, and a constant threat on the left.

Takefusa Kubo — Creative and lively; drifts inside to combine and can unlock defenses with one clever touch.

Wataru Endo — The midfield stabilizer; breaks up play, organizes the press, and adds leadership in big moments.

Daichi Kamada — Smooth, technical operator; times forward runs well and links midfield to attack with control.

Hiroki Ito — A reliable, modern defender; comfortable in possession and strong in duels across the back line.

*Yuto Nagatomo — Japan's tireless full-back; years of experience, consistency, and a defining presence for the national team.

***Maya Yoshida** — Longtime defensive leader; composed, dependable, and central to Japan's identity for over a decade.

Matchday Menu

Appetizers: Edamame.
Main: Order in Sushi (make-your-own is fun, but it should be an activity *before* the game starts).
Dessert: Mochi.
Drink: Sapporo or Sake.

Norway

Norway's football culture is built on humility, hard work, and heart. They don't do drama; they do determination. Every match feels grounded in effort, teamwork, and belief — the Nordic way. The men's team is chasing a long-overdue breakthrough, while the women's team remains one of the pioneers of the sport. In Norway, football isn't about flash. It's about progress, one disciplined pass at a time.

Herstory

The Norwegian women were early trailblazers, winning the 1995 FIFA Women's World Cup and consistent contenders for decades; they were the first European powerhouse in the women's game. For years, they were the team to beat.

Norway's women's team was the blueprint long before others caught up. World Cup winners in 1995 and consistent contenders for decades, they were the first European powerhouse in the women's game. With icons like Hege Riise and Ada Hegerberg, Norway set the standard for excellence, equality, and leadership. They've inspired not just players, but policies — proving what investment in women's football can do.

Trophies & Titles

World Cup Wins (1):
1995 in Sweden vs. Germany
Other Titles:
UEFA Women's Euro: 2 (1987, 1993)
Olympic Gold: 1 (2000)

Legends

Hege Riise — One of the greatest midfielders in women's football history; Euro, World Cup, and Olympic champion.

Gro Espeseth — Defensive rock of Norway's golden generation; tenacious and vital to their titles.

Solveig Gulbrandsen — Elegant, creative midfielder; a driving force through multiple eras and a national icon.

Ada Hegerberg — The first women's Ballon d'Or winner; a generational goalscorer whose impact transcends Norway.

Caroline Graham Hansen — One of the world's elite attackers; technical, brilliant, and a defining star of modern football.

SHIFTING THE SYSTEM

In 2018, Ada Hegerberg became the first woman — and the first Norwegian — to win the Ballon d'Or Féminin, football's highest individual honor. Yet at the height of her career, she walked away from Norway's national team. Her protest wasn't about fame or money — it was about principle. Norway, often praised as a global model for gender equality, was falling short on its own pitch. The women's team faced unequal resources and respect, but Hegerberg's fight ran deeper: she demanded equal investment in girls' academies, coaching, and development — not just equal pay.

Her five-year absence forced the Norwegian Football Federation to confront the gap between its ideals and its reality. Norway became the first nation to introduce an "equal pay" deal for its men's and women's national teams — made possible in part by the men, who collectively redirected 550,000 Norwegian kroner of their earnings to help close the gap. The federation doubled its financial support for the women's side, narrowing the divide — but not erasing it. Hegerberg reminded everyone that the most significant imbalance wasn't financial — it was cultural.

Hegerberg's stand became a mirror for a nation proud of its progress, and her influence reached far beyond football — inspiring women and girls across Norway to expect more, not out of anger, but out of conviction.

Players to Watch

Guro Reiten — Technical, reliable, and deadly from broad areas; one of Norway's most consistent attackers.

Frida Maanum — Dynamic midfielder; creative, physical, and central to Norway's new identity.

Julie Blakstad — Strong, direct winger; brings pace, energy, and attacking intent every time she plays.

Lisa Naalsund — Intelligent, box-to-box midfielder; presses well and links phases smoothly.

Sophie Roman Haug — Clinical, instinctive forward; big-game scorer with excellent positioning.

*****Maren Mjelde** — Veteran defender and long-time leader; calm under pressure and still hugely influential.

*****Ingrid Syrstad Engen** — Versatile midfielder/defender; innovative, composed, and culturally significant in Norway's modern era.

History

Norway's men's team has never quite cracked the global elite, but the horizon looks bright. After making appearances in the World Cup in 1994 and 1998, the country remained quiet for years — until a new generation emerged. With stars like Erling Haaland and Martin Ødegaard leading the charge, Norway's football identity is shifting from modest to mighty. The blueprint is simple: patience, power, and belief that the future belongs to them. If their rise continues, the next Nordic legends may come not from myth, but with thunderous strikes and lightning speed.

Trophies & Titles

World Cup Wins (0):
None, but the next era looks promising.
Other Titles:
None, but the next era looks promising.

Legends

John Arne Riise — Norway's most iconic modern player; powerful left foot, long-range goals, and unmatched longevity.

Ole Gunnar Solskjær — Clinical and composed; a beloved striker known for big moments and lasting global recognition.

Henning Berg — Defensive mainstay; reliable, consistent, and key to Norway's strongest era.

Egil "Drillo" Olsen — Tactical revolutionary and national icon; transformed Norway's identity and success in the 1990s.

Players to Watch

Erling Haaland — A generational striker; explosive power, elite finishing, and the centerpiece of Norway's entire attack.

Martin Ødegaard — Norway's creative leader; smooth on the ball, smart between the lines, and the team's tactical brain.

Alexander Sørloth — A physical, direct forward; complements Haaland with strong hold-up play and reliable finishing.

Antonio Nusa — A promising young winger; quick, confident, and one of Norway's brightest attacking prospects.

Oscar Bobb — A technical, clever playmaker; operates well in tight spaces and adds real creativity on the right.

*****Martin Linnes** — Versatile, dependable, and long-serving; respected veteran presence nearing the end of his international run.

*****Stefan Strandberg** — Physical center-back and experienced leader; part of Norway's backbone during their rebuilding years.

Matchday Menu

Appetizers: Smoked salmon on rye.
Main: Kjøttkaker — Norwegian meatballs.
Dessert: Kransekake.
Drink: Aquavit.

The Netherlands

T he Netherlands, also known as Holland, is one of the most stylish teams in soccer history — and unfortunately, one of the unluckiest. Every pass feels intentional, every movement part of a grander design. Even in defeat, they've shaped how the world plays — thinkers, dreamers, perfectionists in orange. The Dutch are known for their Total Football approach, jaw-dropping orange kits, and heartbreaking losses on the biggest stages.

History

Few nations have defined football as deeply — or suffered as poetically — as the Netherlands. Despite reaching three World Cup finals (1974, 1978, 2010), they've never won one. But their gift to the game, Total Football, changed everything. Under Rinus Michels and Johan Cruyff, they redefined tactics, replacing rigid positions with movement and intelligence. The Dutch became the philosophers of football.

Trophies & Titles

Men's World Cup Wins (0):
> Runners-up:
> 1974 in West Germany vs. West Germany
> 1978 in Argentina vs. Argentina
> 2010 in South Africa vs. Spain

Other Titles:
> UEFA Euro: 1 (1988)
> UEFA Nations League: Runners-up (2019)

Legends

Johan Cruyff — The architect of Dutch football; visionary, elegant, and a global icon who changed the sport.

Marco van Basten — A lethal, graceful striker; unforgettable goals and a defining star of the late '80s.

Ruud Gullit — Powerful, stylish, and versatile; a leader of the Netherlands' golden generation.

Frank Rijkaard — Intelligent and composed; cornerstone of club and country during their most successful era.

Dennis Bergkamp — The master technician; sublime touch, iconic goals, and pure composure on the ball.

Arjen Robben — Everyone knew his move — no one could stop it. Forever known by Mexicans for his theatrical dives.

Ronald Koeman — A defender with playmaker instincts; free-kick threat and key figure in Dutch success.

TOTAL FOOTBALL

The Dutch (the people from Holland) reinvented football. In the 1970s, under coach Rinus Michels and captain Johan Cruyff, the Netherlands introduced Total Football —a style where every player could take on any role. Defenders attacked, forwards defended, and the game flowed like choreography. It demanded intelligence, movement, and trust. Players swapped spaces seamlessly, reading each other's rhythm instead of sticking to rigid roles. Football became less of a sport and more of a symphony.

The soccer sitcom Ted Lasso does a wonderful rendition of it. Feel free to search "Ted Lasso total football scene."

Though the Netherlands famously lost the 1974 World Cup final, their philosophy outlived the defeat. Total Football became the DNA of modern soccer. It has evolved through various styles, from Barcelona's tiki-taka to Manchester City's fluid systems today. The Dutch may not always win, but their ideas have endured.

Edwin van der Sar — The enduring goalkeeper; calm, reliable, and a model of longevity and excellence.

Players to Watch

Virgil van Dijk — A commanding center-back; calm under pressure and the leader of the Dutch defense.

Frenkie de Jong — Smooth and creative; carries the ball through midfield and controls the team's tempo.

Cody Gakpo — Direct and decisive; finds good spaces and provides goals when the Netherlands need them.

Xavi Simons — Energetic and technical; plays between the lines and adds unpredictability in attack.

Denzel Dumfries — A powerful, aggressive wing-back; bursts forward and creates danger with his runs.

Matthijs de Ligt — Strong and experienced; a dependable presence who brings stability in central defense.

Jeremie Frimpong — Fast and fearless on the right; breaks lines with pace and gives the team width.

*__Memphis Depay__ — One of the national team's top scorers; creative, expressive, and influential, now entering the final phase.

*__Georginio Wijnaldum__ — A big-tournament performer; brilliant, dependable, and long central to the Dutch midfield.

Herstory

Dutch women's football has blossomed into one of Europe's most potent forces. Once overlooked, the Oranje women burst onto the global stage by winning the 2017 European Championship at home and reaching the 2019 World Cup final. They play with the same intelligence and creativity that defines Dutch football — but with sharper efficiency. The next step is clear: winning the World Cup they've narrowly missed.

Trophies & Titles

Women's World Cup Wins (0):

Runners-up: 2019 in France vs. USA

Other Titles:

UEFA Women's Euro: 1 (2017)

Legends

Sherida Spitse — The Netherlands' all-time appearances leader; the midfield anchor and cultural pillar behind their rise to European champions.

Daphne Koster — Defensive leader and early architect of Dutch professionalism; foundational across eras.

Vivianne Miedema — A generational scorer with calm brutality; the all-time leading Dutch goalscorer who redefined their attack.

Lieke Martens — The 2017 global best; elegant, technical, and the face of the Netherlands' golden era.

Players to Watch

Jill Roord — Dynamic, intelligent midfielder; finds pockets, scores goals from a distance, and drives the attack.

Jackie Groenen — Press-resistant, smooth midfielder; controls rhythm and links everything.

Esmee Brugts — Rising star on the left; skillful, bold, and a growing force in transition.

Victoria Pelova — Smart, versatile midfielder; technically sharp and increasingly central to the Dutch build-up.

Lineth Beerensteyn — Fast, aggressive winger; creates chaos and stretches defenses.

Wieke Kaptein — Teenage prodigy with remarkable poise; already playing for Chelsea, she reads the game like a veteran and could become the next Dutch midfield general.

Dominique Janssen — Reliable, composed defender; holds the back line together with experience and poise.

***Sari van Veenendaal** — Euro-winning, era-defining goalkeeper; still a respected figure as she moves toward her final chapters.

The Netherlands rewrote the rulebook — and everyone else has been playing catch-up ever since.

Matchday Menu

Appetizers: Bitterballen.
Main: Stroopwafel Burger.
Dessert: Stroopwafels.
Drink: Heineken.

Portugal

Their style blends Latin flair with European discipline, and their passion runs as deep as their Fado music — beautiful, melancholic, and always dramatic. For decades, Portugal was the heartbreak artist of world football: consistently brilliant, rarely rewarded. But the tide turned, and a generation led by Cristiano Ronaldo made the small country feel mighty.

History

Portugal's journey from promise to power is one of persistence. After years of being football's nearly, they claimed their first major trophy at Euro 2016 — a triumph defined by grit, not glamour. Then in 2019, they won the inaugural UEFA Nations League, proving they weren't a one-hit wonder. Their lone World Cup semifinal (2006) remains a national high point, but Portugal's most significant legacy lies in the artistry of its players: Eusebio's grace, Figo's creativity, Ronaldo's relentless perfectionism. They're still searching for that elusive World Cup, but no one doubts their capacity for brilliance. Portugal has the talent to go deep into any tournament.

Trophies & Titles

Men's World Cup Wins (0):
Still chasing their first.
Other Titles:
UEFA Euro: 1 (2016)
UEFA Nations League: 2 (2019, 2025)

Legends

Cristiano Ronaldo — A global superstar; era-defining talent whose goals, longevity, and cultural impact reshaped Portugal's football identity.

Eusébio — Portugal's first global superstar; powerful, elegant, and one of football's greatest goalscorers.

Luís Figo — The face of the Golden Generation; skillful, influential, and a defining winger of his era.

Rui Costa — "The Maestro" is a visionary playmaker whose elegance and creativity shaped Portugal's style.

Deco — A brilliant midfielder; intelligent, composed, and the heartbeat of Portugal's early-2000s rise.

Players to Watch

Bruno Fernandes — Portugal's creative engine; sharp passing, constant movement, and the link between midfield and attack.

Bernardo Silva — Smart and technical; slips into pockets, controls rhythm, and unlocks defenses with precision.

Rúben Dias — The defensive leader; strong in duels, calm on the ball, and central to Portugal's structure.

Rafael Leão — Explosive and unpredictable; beats defenders wide and brings real danger in transition.

Vitinha — Composed and clever; keeps the midfield organized and helps Portugal play with control.

Diogo Jota — Direct and decisive; great movement in the box and a reliable scorer when chances appear.

Gonçalo Ramos — A confident striker; aggressive runs, sharp finishing, and a natural successor up front.

***Cristiano Ronaldo** — Portugal's all-time icon; record-setting scorer and global superstar nearing the end of an extraordinary era.

***Pepe** — A fierce defensive leader; physical, experienced, and still commanding, but in the closing stretch.

Herstory

Portugal's women's team is finally stepping into its own story. Long overshadowed by the men's success, they've built a foundation of resilience and rising talent. Their first World Cup debut was in 2023. The next generation is skillful, fearless, and determined to prove Portugal's artistry isn't limited to one side of the game.

Trophies & Titles

Women's World Cup Wins (0):
2023 marked their first appearance — a milestone in itself.
Other Titles:
None yet, but qualification alone signals the start of something real.

Legends

Cláudia Neto — The trailblazer; Portugal's first global star.

Carla Couto — Veteran goal scorer who paved the way.

Edite Fernandes — Early hero of women's football; relentless and underappreciated.

Players to Watch

Jéssica Silva — Electric winger/forward with flair and pace; the team's biggest creative spark.

Kika Nazareth — Young, elegant playmaker from Benfica; already a leader in midfield and one of Europe's brightest rising stars.

Tatiana Pinto — Steady leader; controls tempo and temperament— Box-to-box midfielder who drives play and connects defense to attack.

Diana Silva — Hardworking striker with a nose for chaos.

Carole Costa — Veteran defender and emotional anchor; brings composure and leadership to a young squad.

Matchday Menu

Appetizers: Pastéis de bacalhau (cod fritters).
Main: Frango piri-piri.
Dessert: Pastel de nata.
Drink: Vinho Verde.

Mexico

Mexican fans show up like the World Cup's already been won — mariachi blaring, face paint flawless, tequila flowing like it's part of the national strategy. And somehow, passion alone still hasn't brought home the golden trophy. Football runs through Mexico's veins. Every match is a celebration; every loss, a national mourning. They're loud, loyal, and heartbreak-hardened — forever stuck between potential and payoff, but their devotion never fades.

History

Hosting the World Cup twice (1970, 1986) and co-hosting again in 2026, Mexico has appeared in 18 World Cups and qualified for every one since 1994. They almost consistently make it to the Round of 16, then their heartbreaks. The nation calls it El Quinto Partido — "the fifth match" — a curse that's lingered since 1986, the last time Mexico reached the quarterfinals.

They've produced generations of brilliance, from Hugo Sánchez to Rafa Márquez, and remain the pride of CONCACAF. Mexico's challenge has never been getting there — it's finally breaking through. Whether it's bad luck, nerves, or a scoreboard that won't cooperate, the fans turn every match into a street parade anyway.

Trophies & Titles

Men's World Cup Wins (0):
Eliminated at the Round of 16 seven times in a row.
Other Titles:
CONCACAF Gold Cup: 12 regional kings of North America).
FIFA Confederations Cup: 1 (1999)

Legends

Hugo Sánchez — Mexico's global superstar; acrobatic finishing, Real Madrid dominance, and the nation's greatest goalscorer.

Rafael Márquez — The general; elegant, intelligent, and one of the finest defenders in CONCACAF history.

Cuauhtémoc Blanco — Creative and fiery; a national icon with unmatched personality and unforgettable moments.

Claudio Suárez — The dependable rock; extraordinary longevity and leadership throughout Mexico's strongest defensive era.

Jorge Campos — The flamboyant, fearless goalkeeper-forward hybrid; a cultural icon whose style transcended the sport.

Players to Watch

Hirving "Chucky" Lozano — Direct and explosive; stretches defenses with pace and brings danger on the counter.

Edson Álvarez — Mexico's midfield anchor; tough in duels, confident on the ball, and central to the team's structure.

Santiago Giménez — A rising striker; sharp movement, strong finishing, and the future of Mexico's attack.

Johan Vásquez — A steady, maturing defender; reliable in big moments and growing into a leadership role.

César Montes — Strong in the air and composed in possession; a key presence at the heart of the back line.

Luis Chávez — Technical and calm; known for clean strikes from distance and control in midfield.

*Guillermo Ochoa — Mexico's World Cup hero; reflex saves, big-stage charisma, and a beloved figure entering his final competitive years.

*Andrés Guardado — Longtime captain; steady, respected, and culturally central, now at the end of an exceptional run.

*Héctor Herrera** — A midfield mainstay; physical, experienced, and influential, but no longer part of the core future cycle.

Herstory

Mexico's women's football scene is growing fast and loud. The creation of the Liga MX Femenil in 2017 provided young players with visibility and a platform, sparking a nationwide surge in talent. Although international results are still developing, the energy and infrastructure are in place — and a new generation is ready to challenge the region's giants.

Trophies & Titles

Women's World Cup Wins (0):
Still chasing history.
Other Titles:
CONCACAF Championship Runners-up: 1 (1998)
CONCACAF Women's Championship: Runners-up 2x (1998, 2010).

Legends

Maribel Domínguez ("Marigol") — Mexico's first global star; clinical, fearless, and the striker who put El Tri Femenil on the map.

Charlyn Corral — A prolific, technically gifted goalscorer; broke barriers in Europe and carried Mexico through multiple eras.

Mónica Ocampo — Skillful creator and big-tournament scorer; author of one of the most iconic goals in Women's World Cup history (2011).

Kenti Robles — Defensive pioneer in Europe; consistent, respected, and a symbol of Mexican excellence abroad.

Players to Watch

Lizbeth Ovalle — Mexico's most dangerous winger; quick, clever, and a consistent attacking threat.

Alice Soto — Teen phenom; fearless dribbler and already one of Mexico's most exciting young midfield talents.

Mayra Pelayo — Rising midfielder; confident on the ball and growing into an essential attacking role.

Jacqueline Ovalle — Direct, energetic, wide attacker; brings spark and unpredictability in the final third.

*****Stephany Mayor** — A modern symbol of El Tri Femenil; culturally important, instantly recognizable, and still influential even as she enters her later years.

*****Kenti Robles** — Still active and still iconic; one of the most respected Mexican players in the world, even as the next generation steps forward.

Matchday Menu

Appetizers: Chips and guacamole.
Main: Tacos al pastor, asada, etc. Whatever you do, not hardshell tacos. Have some respect.
Dessert: Churros.
Drink: Michelada or a Margarita (see page 194 for presentation).

Croatia

For a country with just over 4 million people, Croatia punches way above its weight. Croatia's rise is one of modern football's most remarkable stories. They're the underdogs who refuse to act like it — elegant one moment, ruthless the next. Croatia's style is patient, technical, and intense — and their fans feel everything.

History

Croatia stunned the world in 2018 when they reached the World Cup final — and gave France a serious run for their money (they lost 4–2, but won the world's respect). Then in 2022, they made it all the way to the semi-finals, proving it wasn't a fluke. Emerging as an independent nation in the 1990s, they reached the World Cup semifinals in 1998 — their first appearance — led by Davor Šuker's golden boots. Twenty years later, they advanced even further, reaching the 2018 World Cup final in Russia, where they lost only to France. They followed that up with a third-place finish in 2022, cementing themselves as a small country with a giant heart. Croatia commands respect.

Trophies & Titles

Men's World Cup Wins (0):
Runners-up: 2018 in Russia vs. France
Third Place: 1998 in France, 2022 in Qatar
Other Titles:
None — but eternal overachievers.

Legends

Davor Šuker — Croatia's original superstar; Golden Boot winner in 1998 and their early global face.

Zvonimir Boban — The creative leader of the '98 generation; intelligent, smooth, and culturally influential.

Robert Prosinečki — Elegant and technical; a gifted midfielder whose style left a lasting mark.

Bernard Vukas — Croatia's early icon; brilliant dribbler and widely considered one of the nation's finest talents.

Mario Mandžukić — (Yes, again — dual placement) Tireless forward whose big-stage heroics are woven into Croatia's football identity.

Ivan Rakitić — (Dual placement as well) Key architect of Croatia's midfield success and 2018 World Cup run.

Luka Modrić — A generational midfielder; Ballon d'Or winner who led Croatia to historic heights and redefined what's possible for a small nation.

Players to Watch

Joško Gvardiol — A dominant, modern defender; fast, composed, and the backbone of Croatia's next generation.

Mateo Kovačić — Smooth and press-resistant; carries the ball through midfield and keeps Croatia ticking.

Marcelo Brozović — Croatia's midfield metronome; covers ground, wins duels, and distributes with precision.

Ivan Perišić — Experienced and direct; pops up in big tournaments with clutch goals and hard running.

Andrej Kramarić — A clever, reliable scorer; finds pockets of space and gives Croatia the end product.

*Luka Modrić** — Croatia's most outstanding player; elegant, tireless, and the emotional core of the national team's golden era.

*Ivan Rakitić** — A brilliant technician; key to Croatia's midfield dominance during their peak years.

*Mario Mandžukić** — Powerful and relentless; big-game goals and warrior energy defined Croatia's modern rise.

Herstory

Croatia's women's team is still writing its story — steadily, quietly, with determination. The domestic league is semi-professional, and the national team competes against heavyweights such as Germany, Spain, and England in European qualifiers, making it extremely challenging to break through. Resources and visibility have long lagged behind, but the passion is genuine. The next generation, raised on the success of the men's team, is beginning to dream bigger. Croatia's women may not yet have global trophies, but their foundation is being built by fighters and dreamers alike. The team has been improving slowly, with more players moving abroad to play professionally (especially in Italy and Germany), which could strengthen future campaigns.

Trophies & Titles

Women's World Cup Wins (0):
Still waiting for their first qualification.
Other Titles:
None yet — the journey is just beginning.

Legends

Maja Janković — Midfield mainstay of Croatia's early modern era; consistent, influential, and a leader through the program's toughest years.

Iva Landeka — Creative, composed playmaker; the face of Croatia's midfield for more than a decade and a foundational figure in the national team's identity.

Players to Watch

Ivana Rudelić — Direct, confident forward; one of Croatia's clearest attacking threats.

Ivona Dadić — Energetic midfielder; improving quickly and growing into a central role.

Doris Bačić — Experienced goalkeeper who still shapes matches; steady hands in a team that needs stability.

Matea Bošnjak — Strong, reliable defender; reads the game well and anchors the back line with maturity.

*__Iva Landeka__ — Still active, still a leader, still influential — but her era-defining work is complete.

*__Kristina Ercegović__ — Veteran presence; composed, respected, and entering her late-career chapter with steady influence.

Matchday Menu

Appetizers: Pršut (dry-cured ham)
Main: Ćevapi
Dessert: Kremšnita
Drink: Rakija

Croatia doesn't need a population of millions — just eleven hearts that refuse to quit.

And the Rest?

I f you look closely, only Europe and South America have ever lifted the men's World Cup. But the rest of the world has shaped the tournament's soul just as much — through shock upsets, miracle runs, and the kind of emotional moments that make the sport universal.

Africa

The trophy case may still be empty, but the stories are iconic. Cameroon danced into history in 1990, Ghana nearly rewrote destiny in 2010, and Morocco became the first African semifinalist in 2022. The win hasn't come yet — but the magic already has.

Asia

South Korea's 2002 semifinal run announced Asia's arrival, and Japan has quietly become a model of discipline and technical brilliance. Even their fans clean the stadium afterward — proof that respect can be a sporting philosophy.

The Middle East

Qatar 2022 brought the region its first World Cup, and Saudi Arabia's shock upset over Argentina became an instant global headline. With local leagues investing billions and drawing international stars, the Middle East is shaping soccer's future as much as its present.

North America

Mexico qualifies like it's a birthright, but often falls at the Round of 16. The U.S. men have had flashes, while the U.S. women are a dynasty with four World Cups. Canada is the promising newcomer — and co-hosting in 2026 puts it squarely on the map.

These regions may not have a star above their crest yet, but they've already given the World Cup some of its most unforgettable chapters. And when one of them finally wins, it will feel less like an upset and more like history balancing itself out.

You don't have to memorize an atlas of football nations. This book has already given you more than enough to keep up (and, frankly, to impress). The rest is just geography and logistics... which even FIFA struggles with.

VI.
for a homefield advantage

Hosting

Romance isn't all sunshine and rainbows.
Sometimes it's wings and fries.

For many men, the way to their heart is through their stomach. This does not mean you have to go all Martha Stewart on him. Ordering out is just as effective, just a little less fun. This chapter outlines the dos and don'ts of your average Soccer Cuisine!

Step 1 — Ensure the game is viewable.

If you're hosting, the TV/stream/login/cables/speaker situation must be resolved before guests arrive. You can absolutely delegate this to your partner, but "I'll do it later" is not acceptable if it's less than an hour before kickoff. ENSURE it gets done before guests arrive.

Step 2 — Protect your furniture.

Do not rely on guests to be neat. They will not be tidy. It is preferable to display a cheap plastic tablecloth that will protect your antiques or IKEA valuables. A washable throw or a "sacrificial couch blanket" is also in play. This prevents most hostesses from having a mini panic attack.

Step 3 — Recognize the amount of time and energy you can expend on hosting

Decide the level of energy you and your partner have for this. Ordering in pizza will not change the result of the game (although having ice cream could soften the blow after a loss). Strategize and negotiate the clean up as part of the planning.

Choose between:

Ordering in (pizza, wings, etc.) — low effort but well received.

Store-bought — you "assembled," not "cooked," still appreciated!

Potluck style — outsource the labor, keep the credit. Make sure you can handle the logistics.

Build-your-own stations — tacos, sliders, nachos.

Martha-Stewart mode — homemade dips, themed cupcakes, and artisanal garnish (only do this if you enjoy it; don't do it for the oohs and ahs, those are reserved for the players).

This book admires Martha Stewart, but is not affiliated.

Step 4 — Pick your menu

Game Changer: Look at the World Cup section for country-specific menu ideas.

Appetizers and Sides

Crackers and Dips (hummus)

Fries or Potato Wedges

Cold Cuts / Deli Meats Platter

Mixed Nuts or Spiced Nuts

Vegetable Platter + Dip (ranch, hummus, etc.)

Mini Sandwiches / Sliders

Chicken Wings

Onion Rings

Mozzarella Sticks / Cheese Bites

Stuffed Pastry Bites (samosa, empanada, puff pastry, etc.)

Popcorn (various seasonings)

Flatbread or Mini Pizza Slices

Pretzels (soft or crunchy)

Sausage Bites / Cocktail Sausages

Chips (salsa, bean dip, spinach dip)

Main Dishes

Mini sandwiches

Pizza slices/flatbreads

Burgers

Mini meat or veggie pies

Skewers (meat, tofu, veggie)

Taquitos/spring rolls

Hot dogs/sausages in buns

Chicken wings or drumettes (with a napkin plan)

Meatball subs (small + tight, not overloaded)

Stuffed breads (calzones, empanadas, pupusas, Jamaican patties)

"Build your own" taco bar, burrito bar, nacho bar... You get the point.

Drinks

Beer

Cocktails

Soft Drinks

Water

Coffee/Tea

Dessert

- Brownie bites
- Cookie assortment
- Churro bites/donut holes
- Rice Krispies treats
- Chocolate-covered pretzels
- Baklava bites
- Turkish delight squares
- Mochi ice cream
- Frozen dessert bites
- Store-bought ice cream sandwiches
- Ice cream sundae bar
- Mini waffle station
- Decorate-your-own cupcakes
- Black + white cake pops
- Black and white muffins
- Cupcakes with team-colored frosting
- Costco sheet cake (cut into tiny squares, no shame)
- Chocolate soccer balls
- "Red card" Jell-O shots
- Paletas/popsicles
- Store bought brownies with powdered sugar on top look homemade
- Fruit skewers with mint
- Lemon sorbet cups

Once food, drinks, and functional streaming are set, the other details are for you. Most partners do not care for themed ideas or presentations.
But doing them can be fun!

Step 5 — Pick your decorations

Themed Ideas

International

Flavors: Celebrate the global nature of soccer with foods from different countries like Italian pizza, Mexican tacos, German pretzels, and Brazilian brigadeiros. Go back to the World Cup section for country-specific ideas!

Team Colors: Create dishes in the colors of the teams playing — for example, red and white cupcakes for a team with those colors.

DIY Food Stations: Let guests customize their own food, like a build-your-own burger, taco bar, margarita bar, or sangria bar.

Presentation Tips

Soccer-Themed Decorations: Use soccer-themed plates, napkins, and tablecloths.

Labeling: Label foods with soccer-themed names or tags.

Convenience: Provide a sufficient number of napkins, plates, and utensils to make it easy for guests to serve themselves.

Finger Foods: Offer lots of finger foods that are easy to eat without missing the action.

Find other great ideas here!

Author may earn a small commission at no extra cost to you.

A make-your-own margarita station is an easy way to entertain guests without actually doing much. Lay a discardable tablecloth and write each step around the table — shakers, juices, spirits, ice, rims, garnishes — and let guests follow the path around the table like a mini cocktail course. It keeps the traffic moving, keeps you out of bartender jail, and makes everyone feel like they're part of the fun instead of waiting in line for a drink. This also works for sangrias, food like nachos, tacos, or any buffet-style setup.

Add some ice

Shake! Shake! Shake! Shake!

Add a shot

Pick a glass

Choose your juice

Salt your Rim

Pour and garnish

Start Here!

Pick a shaker (mason jar)

Gift Guide

$$$$	Season tickets
$$$$	Signed memorabilia (ball, boots, jersey)
$$$$	Foosball Table
$$$–$$$$	Noise-canceling headphones
$$$–$$$$	Projector + portable screen
$$$	Quality cooler (Yeti, Igloo)
$$$	Official team jersey (club or national)
$$$	Custom jersey with their name/number
$$$	Limited edition World Cup ball replica
$$$	Upgraded soundbar
$$$	Game day soccer fan gift basket (snacks and drinks, team merch)
$$$	Mini foosball table
$$$	LEGO stadium set (Old Trafford, Camp Nou, etc.)
$$$	Mini-fridge
$$–$$$	Tickets to a local game (MLS, NWSL, or international friendlies)
$$	Snack subscription box (international snacks)
$$	High-quality soccer ball (Adidas, Nike, Puma)
$$	Whiskey stones/decanter set
$$	Streaming stick (Roku, Firestick, Apple TV)
$$	Soccer video games (FIFA, Football Manager)
$$	Portable pop-up goal for backyard play
$$	Backpack or duffel bag
$–$$$	Collectible soccer trading cards
$–$$	Subscription to a soccer magazine or streaming service

$–$$ Themed home décor (wall art, posters, stadium prints)

$–$$ Comfy team colored athleisure wear

$–$$ Stadium blanket for match days

$–$$ Universal remote

$–$$ Reusable insulated tumblers

$-$$ Panini World Cup cards and stickers (World Cup Album)

$ Biography of their soccer legend (Messi, Ronaldo, Pele, Megan Rapinoe)

$ Soccer scarf (classic supporter style)

$ Personalized soccer mug or pint glass

$ Match-day beanie or cap

$ Personalized beer steins/pint glasses

$ Customized phone case with team colors

$ Soccer-themed socks or slippers

$ Soccer trivia game or card set

Legend:

$= under $25 USD

$$= $25 - $75 USD

$$$= $75 - $200 USD

$$$$= + $200 USD

Find other great ideas here!

Author may earn a small
commission at no extra cost to you.

Chores While Watching TV

I t's hard to keep your cool when there is a mountain of things that need to be done, and your partner decides to cope with all of it by checking out with a 2-hour game. Although he might need the break, it does not alleviate the situation.

Don't hold back when you are feeling overwhelmed. Name the feeling (see page # for a refresher) and ask for a brainstorming session on how to tackle that mountain of to-dos.

Ideally, you will address and schedule the "important" tasks during your "Game Plan for the Week" meetings. This will ease the tension around avoidable conflicts. But life happens, timing gets messy, and sometimes he will need to contribute during a game. There are only so many hours in a day, and if he needs to pick up his slack during game time, here are a few activities he can do while watching the game.

Important note: this applies to regular games — not championship finals, rivalry derbies, or anything that turns him into a stand-up-shout-at-the-TV version of himself. If he's locked in like it's a national emergency, let the game finish and then tag him back in. Timing is a crucial component of strategy. Emotional messes do not pair well with productivity.

A good rule of thumb is, **if he can scroll Instagram, then he can:**

☐ Brush pets
☐ Sort mail or paperwork

- ☐ Wrap presents
- ☐ Label or back up digital files
- ☐ Organize digital files/photos
- ☐ Pay bills - automate bill payment
- ☐ Opt out of unwanted subscriptions
- ☐ Wipe down remotes and keyboards
- ☐ Defuzz sweaters with a lint shaver
- ☐ Shred old documents*
- ☐ Sort cables/chargers into labeled bags or ties
- ☐ Dust around the living room
- ☐ Match and fold socks
- ☐ Trim indoor plants*
- ☐ Prepare pet food
- ☐ Wipe plant leaves
- ☐ Grate cheese*
- ☐ Online shopping
- ☐ Iron clothes
- ☐ Fold laundry

☐ Order takeout!

☐ Clean pet toys or food bowl

☐ Clean out and organize drawers

☐ Shell peas or smashing beans/potatoes

☐ Declutter items (e.g., sorting through books, DVDs, or supplies)

☐ Light exercise: Make a burpee when the other team steals the ball.

☐ Sort pantry items or spices - throwing away expired ones

☐ Roll change into paper coin wrappers (satisfying too)

☐ Meal-prep snacks like chopping veggies or portioning trail mix nuts

☐ Refill household items (soap dispensers, salt/pepper shakers)

☐ Polish shoes, clean his sneakers, or other small items

☐ Purge his closet - make seasonal piles and donate piles (out-of-season clothing goes in a box under the bed or in storage).

*Disclaimer: avoid sharp objects unless he can ACTUALLY take his eyes off the screen

Grounding Techniques

Sensory (External Awareness)

5-4-3-2-1 Technique

Name: 5 things you can see
4 things you can touch
3 things you can hear
2 things you can smell
1 thing you can taste

Hold a Cold Drink or an Ice Cube

Let the sensation bring your focus to the present moment.

Touch Textured Objects

Feel the grain of a wooden table, the ridges of your phone case, or the texture of your clothes.

Step Outside

Fresh air, the sun on your skin, or the sound of traffic/noise can help snap you back into your body.

Movement-Based (Action-Oriented)

Take a 5-Minute Walk

No phone, no music — just pay attention to your footsteps and surroundings.

Controlled Breathing

Try box breathing: Inhale 4 seconds
Hold 4 seconds
Exhale 4 seconds
Hold 4 seconds
Repeat 4–5 rounds.

Do a Simple Task

Fold laundry, wash dishes, or organize your desk. Engaging in a low-stakes, physical activity helps bring your mind back to the basics.

Cognitive (Mind-Based)

Count Backwards from 100 by 3s

It gives your mind something to focus on and pulls attention away from stress. Sudoku or crossword puzzles function similarly.

Name Categories

Pick a category (sports teams, car brands, cities) and name as many as you can.

Repeat a Phrase

Example: "I am here. I am okay. This will pass." Repeating a calm truth helps reduce spiraling thoughts.

Check the Facts

What do I know for sure?
What is my brain assuming?
What's actually happening right now?

Physical (Body-Based)

Cold Water Reset

Splash cold water on your face or run your wrists under cold water. It helps activate the parasympathetic nervous system and slow racing thoughts.

Push Against a Wall

Place both hands flat on a wall and gently push for 10–15 seconds. Feel your strength and connection to something solid.

Squeeze Something

Grip a stress ball, a rolled towel, or even your own fist for a few seconds, then release slowly. Repeat.

Tense and Release

Tense one muscle group at a time (like your shoulders or fists), hold for 5 seconds, then release. Work your way down your body.

Weighted Blanket or Compression

If at home, sitting under a weighted blanket or wearing a snug hoodie can create a calming, grounding effect.

Overall quality & watch-worthiness ★

Soccer knowledge required ⚽

TV Guide

Movies

Escape to Victory (1981) ⚽ ★★★★★⭒
A WWII sports drama about Allied prisoners of war playing a football match against a German team (starring young Sylvester Stallone & Pelé).

The Damned United (2009) ⚽⚽ ★★★★★★
A dramatized portrayal of Brian Clough's brief and notorious tenure as manager of Leeds United.

Bend It Like Beckham (2002) ⚽ ★★★★★⭒
A coming-of-age comedy-drama about a young British-Indian woman who secretly plays soccer against her parents' wishes.

Goal! The Dream Begins (2005) ⚽⚽ ★★★★★★
A sports drama following a young player's journey from amateur football to a professional opportunity in Europe.

Goal II: Living the Dream (2007) ⚽⚽ ★★★★★
A sequel following the main character's move to Real Madrid and the challenges of fame and elite-level football.

Goal II: Living the Dream (2007) ⚽⚽ ★★★★★★
A sequel following the main character's move to Real Madrid and the challenges of fame and elite-level football.

Pelé: Birth of a Legend (2016)
A dramatized biopic about Pelé's early life leading up to his breakthrough at the 1958 World Cup.

The Beautiful Game (2024)
A drama about a coach guiding a team of homeless footballers preparing for the Homeless World Cup.

The Miracle of Bern (2003)
A drama centered around Germany's unexpected victory in the 1954 World Cup, seen through a family's perspective (German, subtitles).

Shaolin Soccer (2001)
A comedy blending martial arts and soccer, where a former monk assembles a team using kung-fu skills to play football.

Next Goal Wins (2023 film)
A fictionalized comedic retelling of the same American Samoa story, directed by Taika Waititi.

Next Goal Wins (2014 doc)
A documentary following the American Samoa national team as they attempt to recover from a 31–0 World Cup qualifying loss.

Green Street Hooligans (2005)
A drama focused on football hooliganism within West Ham's supporter culture, rather than the sport itself.

Offside (2006)
An Iranian film about girls who attempt to enter a men's World Cup qualifying match despite restrictions banning them from stadiums (Persian, subtitles).

TV Shows

Ted Lasso (2020–2023)
Pure serotonin, found family, emotional gut-punches in tracksuits. Healthy masculinity is on full display. If you watch anything... Please watch Ted Lasso.

The English Game (2020)
A historical miniseries about the early development of modern football in England, focusing on class divisions and the sport's evolution. *Trigger warning*: This film briefly includes a storyline involving miscarriage.

Club de Cuervos (2015–2019) ⚽⚽★★★★★★
A Mexican dramedy following a brother–sister power struggle as they fight for control of a professional soccer club after their father dies (Spanish, with subtitles).

Dream Team (1997–2007) ⚽⚽⚽★★★★★
A long-running British drama centered around a fictional Premier League club, blending on-field events with personal and club scandals.

Maradona: Blessed Dream (2021) ⚽★★★★★★
A sweeping dramatized series chronicling Diego Maradona's meteoric rise, chaotic genius, and explosive life on and off the pitch. Emotional, gripping, and essential for understanding why some fans treat him like a religion.

Baggio: The Divine Ponytail (2021) ⚽⚽★★★★
A biographical drama depicting the career and personal struggles of Italian football legend Roberto Baggio (Italian, subtitles).

Blue Lock (Anime, 2022–) ⚽★★★★★
A high-intensity sports anime about a radical training program designed to create Japan's ultimate striker through extreme competition (Japanese, subtitles or dubbed).

The First Team (2020) ⚽★★★★
A comedy about three young players navigating the politics, egos, and absurdity of life inside a professional football club.

Ballers (2015–2019) ⚽★★★★★
A sports-business dramedy centered on athletes' financial management and off-field lives; not soccer-specific but includes football culture.

Documentaries / Docuseries

All or Nothing Series ⚽⚽★★★★★★
Documentaries give behind-the-scenes access to professional soccer teams' seasons, offering insight into training, strategy, and management.

Beckham (2023) ⚽★★★★★
A docuseries covering David Beckham's life, career, fame, and personal challenges, spanning his evolution on and off the pitch..

Welcome to Wrexham (2022–) ⚽★★★★★
A docuseries following the takeover of a Welsh football club by Ryan Reynolds and Rob McElhenney, documenting the club's rebuild.

Sunderland 'Til I Die (2018–2020) ⚽★★★★★★
A documentary series tracking Sunderland AFC through turbulent seasons marked by relegation battles and financial instability.

This Is Football (Amazon, 2019) ⚽★★★★★★
A global documentary series exploring the cultural, emotional, and social impact of football across different countries.

Ronaldo (2015) ⚽⚽★★★★★
A polished and intimate portrait of Cristiano Ronaldo at the height of his career, blending family dynamics, fame, and the relentless pressure of elite football.

Diego Maradona (2019) ⚽⚽★★★★★★
A documentary on the life of Diego Maradona,includes real footage of games and intervies.Displays the complications of fame and portrays intricate layers of Machismo in Latin American cultures.

The Two Escobars (2010) (Spanish, subtitles) ⚽⚽★★★★★★
A documentary linking Colombian footballer Andrés Escobar with drug lord Pablo Escobar, examining the intersection of soccer and cartel politics.

Take the Ball, Pass the Ball (2018) ⚽⚽⚽★★★★★★
A documentary about FC Barcelona's era under Pep Guardiola, exploring their tactics, philosophy, and dominance.

Sir Alex Ferguson: Never Give In (2021) ⚽⚽★★★★★★
A documentary recounting the career, leadership, and personal history of Manchester United's long-time manager.

Captains (2022) ⚽⚽★★★★★
A FIFA-backed series following national team captains from several countries as they prepare for World Cup qualification (many languages, with subtitles).

The Class of '92 (2013) ⚽⚽★★★★★★
A film documenting six Manchester United academy graduates who rose to prominence together in the 1990s. Beckham, Giggs, Scholes, Neville, all before fame swallowed them.

Speaking his Language

For a Pep Talk

"Every disadvantage has its advantage." – Hendrik Johannes Cruijff.

"The game is not over till the whistle blows. Meaning don't give up. Never give up."

I learned a long time ago that there is something worse than missing the goal, and that's not pulling the trigger. - Mia Hamm

"The first 90 minutes are the most important." – Sir Robert William.

"Winners are not people who never fail, but people who never quit." - Unknown.

"You miss 100% of the goals you don't shoot." – Wayne Gretzky.

For a Heated Discussion

We need a game plan so this doesn't happen to us again.

That reaction was out of bounds.

That's not how I remember the play-by-play. Here is how I experienced it...

Basic Terms

Nil: Zero goals. For example, they lost three-nil.

Pitch: The soccer field.

Goal: The structure a player aims to get the ball into to score points.

Goalkeeper (or Goalie): The player who guards the goal.

Defender: Players positioned near their own goal to stop the opposing team from scoring.

Fear: Is not in the dictionary.

Midfielder: Players who play both offense and defense, typically positioned in the middle of the field.

Forward (or Striker): Players who are primarily responsible for scoring goals.

Kickoff: The start or restart of play from the center of the pitch.

Corner Kick: A free kick taken from the corner of the pitch, awarded to the attacking team when the ball goes out of play off a defender.

Free Kick: A kick awarded to a team following a foul or infringement by the opposing team.

Penalty Kick: A kick taken from the penalty spot, awarded after a foul in the penalty area.

Offside: A rule violation where an attacking player is nearer to the opponent's goal line than both the ball and the second-last opponent when the ball passes to them.

Throw-In: A method of restarting play when the ball goes out of bounds, thrown in from the sidelines.

Yellow Card: A caution issued to a player for unsporting behavior.

Red Card: A dismissal issued to a player for serious foul play, resulting in ejection from the game.

Hat-Trick: When a player scores three goals in a single match.

Clean Sheet: When the goalkeeper or team prevents the opposing team from scoring.

Advanced Terms

Bicycle Kick: An acrobatic kick where the player strikes the ball while airborne and facing away from the goal.

Counter-Attack: A quick transition from defense to offense after regaining possession.

Dribbling: Maneuvering the ball past opponents using individual skill.

Nutmeg: Passing the ball between an opponent's legs.

Marking: Defending against an opponent to prevent them from receiving the ball.

Tiki-Taka: A style of play involving short passing and movement, maintaining possession.

Pressing: A defensive tactic where players apply pressure on the ball carrier.

Sweeper: A defender who roams the defensive line to clear loose balls.

Through Ball: A pass that goes through the defense to a teammate.

Transition: the instant the team switches from defense to attack.

Set Piece: A planned play executed during a free kick, corner kick, or throw-in.

Volley: Kicking the ball while it is in the air.

Half-Volley: Striking the ball immediately after it bounces.

Formation: The tactical arrangement of players on the pitch (e.g., 4-4-2, 3-5-2).

Man-to-Man Marking: A defensive strategy where each player is responsible for marking a specific opponent.

Zonal Marking: A defensive strategy where each player covers a specific area of the pitch.

Equalizer: A goal that ties the game.

Fun Phrases

"**Boot It**": Urging a player to kick the ball hard and far.

"**Gaffer**": A colloquial English term for the team's manager or coach.

"**Hand of God**": A famous, controversial goal scored by Diego Maradona using his hand. Worth a YouTube search.

"**Keeper's Ball**": Shouted by the goalkeeper to claim possession.

"**On the Ball**": In possession of the ball and ready to make a play.

"**Park the Bus**": A strategy where a team defends with many players to protect a lead. More of an English term.

"**Row Z**" or "**Row Zed**": Kicking the ball far out of play, often into the stands, to clear it from danger.

"**Stoppage Time**": Additional time added at the end of a half to make up for delays.

"**The Beautiful Game**": A popular term referring to the sport of soccer.

There are few things you can change about a man...
Their love for soccer isn't one of them.

How Was It?

IDEAS

What would you like the next edition to focus on?

What was **missing?**

What would be **helpful?**

What should we **keep?**

Every comment will be read and used to
improve upcoming editions!

Public Resources

Gambling Support

National Council on Problem Gambling (NCPG) – U.S.

24/7 Helpline: 1-800-522-4700 (GAMBLER)

 - Confidential, available in all 50 states. Offers text and chat options, immediate crisis support, and referrals to local therapists or programs.

Gamblers Anonymous (GA)

A free, peer-support 12-step program for people struggling with gambling behaviors.

 - In-person and online meetings

 - Anonymous, community-focused

 - Good for people who resonate with group accountability

SMART Recovery (Self-Management and Recovery Training)

A science-based alternative to 12-step programs.

 - Focuses on coping skills, emotional regulation, and healthy habits

 - Online meetings, forums, and worksheets

 - Great for people who want tools rather than a spiritual model

Gam-Anon

Support groups specifically for partners and family members of someone with a gambling problem.

 - Emotional support without blame

 - Helps you build boundaries, clarity, and resilience

 - A powerful resource when the partner is struggling but not ready to change yet

State-Level Problem Gambling Programs

Most states offer free or low-cost counseling for gambling through:

- State gambling commissions
- Mental health departments
- Medicaid-funded treatment programs

(Search "[Your State] problem gambling services" — the NCPG site links to each.)

International Resources

- UK: GamCare (24/7 helpline + online tools)
- Canada: Canada Safety Council + provincial helplines
- Australia: Gambling Help Online
- New Zealand: PGF Services (Problem Gambling Foundation)

Financial + Legal Support

Sometimes gambling or substance issues intersect with financial stress or legal risk. These resources help stabilize the "practical" side:

National Foundation for Credit Counseling (NFCC) (nfcc.org)

Legal Aid Services

Available in every state

For situations involving DUIs, custody concerns, or safety plans (lsc. gov).

Alcohol & Substance Use Support Resources

When alcohol or substance use starts affecting emotional safety, reliability, or connection, it may help to explore support. None of these resources require labels or rock-bottom moments — they're simply places where people go to get clarity, community, or direction. These resources are for informational purposes only and are not a substitute for professional medical, legal, or mental health advice.

Alcohol Support (for individuals)

Alcoholics Anonymous (AA)

Global, peer-led meetings offering connection and support.

In-person, online, and phone options (aa.org).

SMART Recovery

Science-based program focused on self-management and behavior change.

Great for people who prefer structure without spirituality (smartrecovery.org).

Moderation Management (MM)

Focuses on reducing alcohol use, not necessarily abstaining.

Helpful for those exploring new habits (moderation.org).

Rethinking Drinking (NIAAA – U.S.)

Evidence-based tools for evaluating drinking patterns.

Anonymous self-assessments (rethinkingdrinking.niaaa.nih.gov).

Hello Sunday Morning / Daybreak Program

Digital community for people taking breaks from alcohol.

Australia-based but widely available (hellosundaymorning.org).

Support for Partners, Family, or Loved Ones

Al-Anon Family Groups

Support for people affected by someone else's drinking.

Helpful for understanding boundaries, enabling patterns, and emotional safety (al-anon.org).

SMART Recovery Family & Friends

Tools for partners and relatives using evidence-based communication practices (smartrecovery.org/family).

NAMI Family Support Groups

Broader mental health focus, but great if substance use overlaps with anxiety, depression, or stress (nami.org).

Substance Use Support (beyond alcohol)

SAMHSA National Helpline (U.S.)

> Free, confidential, 24/7

> Provides treatment referrals and crisis support 1-800-662-HELP (4357).

Shatterproof / ATLAS

> A digital platform helping people find quality substance use treatment.

> Transparent reviews and outcomes (shatterproof.org).

Partnership to End Addiction

> Resources and helplines for families.

> Text/chat support (drugfree.org)

Narcotics Anonymous (NA)

> > Peer-led meetings for those struggling with drugs (na.org).

SMART Recovery (Substances)

> Evidence-based program for any addictive behavior (smartrecovery.org).

Harm Reduction Resources

Not everyone is aiming for abstinence; these support safer use.

Harm Reduction Coalition (harmreduction.org)

Never Use Alone Hotline

> For people who may be using substances in isolation

Trained responders help prevent overdose fatalities (neverusealone.com).

Professional Support Options

Certified Addiction Counselors (CAC)

Searchable directories through state boards or NAADAC (naadac.org).

Psychology Today – Addiction Therapist Directory

Filter by specialty, approach, cost, and insurance (psychologytoday.com).

Telehealth Recovery Programs (many people prefer the privacy and flexibility).

Tempest (alcohol-free lifestyle coaching)

Boulder Care - substance use + medical support. (boulder.care)

Lionrock (online outpatient treatment) - hotline: (800) 495-2282

About the Author

L et's clear up a few things: I am not a soccer fan, lover of a soccer fan, or a therapist. And I'm definitely not here to tell anyone how to run their love life. This book was shaped over the course of two years through hundreds of conversations with customers sharing stories across the counter: frustrations, joy, burnout, miscommunication, and the emotional ripple effects of soccer fandom in their homes. Some were partners of devoted fans. Others *were* the fans. Together, those conversations shaped much of what appears in this book.

Before writing this, I spent seven years working in the counter-sex trafficking field. Unsurprisingly, I burned out. But those years taught me to appreciate the subtleties of healthy dynamics. They're quiet, often overlooked, and incredibly impactful. During that time — and ever since — I've spent years in therapy, learning about tools I wish I'd had long ago.

We need more good in this world. So I turned those lessons into something more tangible: scripts, examples, boundaries, and mindset shifts that real people can actually use. I believe **emotional clarity shouldn't live only inside therapy offices or textbooks.** It belongs in everyday culture, so I have compiled these tools in a format that doesn't make you tune out.

To be clear: this book is not a substitute for therapy. It's not trying to be. Therapy is powerful, sacred work. What this book offers instead is accessible language and perspective — the scripts, the language, the mindset shifts to help you understand yourself and your relationship a little better. Some psychological concepts referenced throughout this book are based on commonly understood clinical principles and are not intended as therapy or clinical guidance.

This isn't a psychologist's guide to loving a sports fanatic. It's a friend's guide to understanding what's happening when your partner seems more emotionally invested in a team than in your weekend plans.

You won't find perfect answers here. But you will find perspective, clarity, and — hopefully — some relief. You're not alone, and you're not overreacting if you feel a little invisible during game season.

I wrote this for you — for all of us trying to love well, stay sane, and hold onto ourselves in relationships that are passionate, messy, but still worth showing up for.

www.ingramcontent.com/pod-product-compliance
Lightning Source LLC
Chambersburg PA
CBHW052018030426
42335CB00026B/3184